THE AIR FRYE
COOKBOOK FOR
AUTHENTIC BRITISH
EVERYDAY FOODS

Inspiring, Healthy, UK Recipes With An Air-Fried Twist Using Metric Measurements

With Colour Pictures

KATHRYNE R. BROOKS

| EDITOR: LYN | INTERIOR DESIGN: FAIZAN |
| COVER ART: ABR | FOOD STYLIST: JO |

Table of Contents

Introduction

With the rise in popularity of air fryers in recent years, it has become clear that consumers are looking for healthier ways to cook their favorite dishes. Many people are also interested in exploring new cuisines and trying out traditional recipes from different parts of the world. In this context, there is a growing demand for cookbooks that cater to these needs, especially those that offer authentic recipes from various cultures.

One such cuisine that has gained a lot of attention in recent years is British cuisine. While it may not be known for its health benefits, there are many classic British dishes that can be adapted to suit a healthier lifestyle, especially with the use of an air fryer. This is where an air fryer cookbook with authentic British recipes and metric measurements can fill a gap in the market and meet the needs of customers who are looking for a healthier way to enjoy their favorite British foods.

Whether it's fish and chips, shepherd's pie, or roast lamb, there are many British classics that can be adapted to an air fryer, without sacrificing flavor or texture. This cookbook will provide readers with a variety of recipes that are not only delicious but also healthier than their traditional counterparts.

Chapter 1
Explanation of Air Fryer Cooking

Air fryer cooking is a method of cooking that uses hot air to circulate around the food, similar to a convection oven. The air is heated by a heating element and then circulated by a fan, which cooks the food evenly and quickly. Air fryers can be used to fry, bake, grill, and roast a variety of foods using little to no oil. This makes air frying a healthier alternative to traditional deep frying, as it significantly reduces the amount of oil needed to achieve crispy and delicious results. Air fryers are also convenient and easy to use, making them a popular kitchen appliance for busy home cooks.

Benefits of Using An Air Fryer for Cooking British Foods

There are several benefits to using an air fryer for cooking British foods. First and foremost, air fryers use hot air to cook food, which means you can achieve the crispy texture of fried food without the need for excessive oil. This is a healthier alternative to traditional deep-frying methods, which can add unnecessary calories and fat to your meals.

Additionally, air fryers are known for their speed and efficiency. They can cook food faster than traditional ovens, and because they use convection heat, the food is cooked evenly on all sides. This means you can spend less time in the kitchen and more time enjoying your delicious British meal.

Air fryers are also very versatile and can be used to cook a wide range of British foods, from classic dishes like fish and chips and shepherd's pie to more modern recipes like crispy baked tofu "chicken" nuggets and vegetable toad in the hole. With an air fryer, you can explore new culinary horizons while still enjoying the traditional tastes of Britain.

Explanation of Metric Measurements and Their Importance

Metric measurements are a system of measurement used in most countries around the world, including the United Kingdom. It is a decimal-based system that uses standard units of measurement for weight, volume, and length.

The importance of using metric measurements in cooking is that it provides a precise and accurate way to measure ingredients, which is essential for achieving consistent results in recipes. It also makes it easier to scale recipes up or down, especially when cooking for a large or small group of people.

Using metric measurements in cooking also makes it easier to follow recipes from different countries, as many countries use the metric system. Additionally, it helps avoid confusion and mistakes when working with recipes that use multiple units of measurement, such as teaspoons and tablespoons, ounces and cups, or Fahrenheit and Celsius.

Brief History of British Cuisine

British cuisine has a long and fascinating history that spans centuries. Traditional British cuisine has been influenced by numerous factors, including the availability of ingredients, the influence of other cultures, and historical events. In the past, British cuisine was often considered plain and unadventurous, but today it has evolved into a diverse and dynamic cuisine that draws on a wide range of influences.

Historically, British cuisine was heavily influenced by the availability of ingredients. For example, fish has always been an important part of the British diet due to the country's proximity to the sea. The introduction of new ingredients from around the world through trade and exploration also had a significant impact on British cuisine. The spice trade, for example, brought a range of new flavors and ingredients to the country.

During the industrial revolution, changes in society also had an impact on British cuisine. As people moved from rural areas to urban centers, food production became more industrialized, and people's diets began to change. Convenience foods, such as canned goods and pre-packaged meals, became more popular.

In recent years, there has been a renewed interest in traditional British cuisine, with a focus on fresh, locally sourced ingredients and classic dishes such as fish and chips, shepherd's pie, and roast beef. Today, British cuisine is known for its comfort food, hearty dishes, and use of high-quality, seasonal ingredients.

Chapter 2
How To Use This Cookbook

Explanation of Recipe Format

Recipe format typically includes a title, introduction, ingredients list, equipment list, instructions, and serving suggestions.

The title should clearly and concisely describe the dish.

The introduction should provide a brief overview of the dish, including its origins or any interesting facts about it.

The ingredients list should include all the necessary ingredients, along with their precise measurements.

The equipment list should specify any special kitchen tools or appliances required to make the dish, such as an air fryer or food processor.

The instructions should be written in a clear, concise, and chronological order, detailing each step required to prepare the dish.

Serving suggestions should offer ideas for how to serve or pair the dish with other foods.

Tips for Successful Air Fryer Cooking

Here are some tips for successful air fryer cooking:

Preheat your air fryer before cooking to ensure even heat distribution and optimal results.

Use cooking spray or a light coating of oil to prevent food from sticking to the air fryer basket or tray.

Don't overcrowd the air fryer basket or tray. Leave enough space between each piece of food to allow for proper air circulation.

Shake or flip food halfway through the cooking process to ensure even cooking and browning.

Adjust cooking times and temperatures based on the size and thickness of the food being cooked.

Use a food thermometer to ensure that meat and poultry are cooked to a safe internal temperature.

Clean your air fryer regularly to prevent buildup of food residue and to ensure optimal performance.

Measurement Conversion Chart

Volume Equivalents (Dry)

US STANDARD	METRIC (APPROXIMATE)
1/8 teaspoon	0.5 mL
1/4 teaspoon	1 mL
1/2 teaspoon	2 mL
3/4 teaspoon	4 mL
1 teaspoon	5 mL
1 tablespoon	15 mL
1/4 cup	59 mL
1/2 cup	118 mL
3/4 cup	177 mL
1 cup	235 mL
2 cups	475 mL
3 cups	700 mL
4 cups	1 L

Volume Equivalents (Liquid)

US STANDARD	US STANDARD (OUNCES)	METRIC (APPROXIMATE)
2 tablespoons	1 fl.oz.	30 mL
1/4 cup	2 fl.oz.	60 mL
1/2 cup	4 fl.oz.	120 mL
1 cup	8 fl.oz.	240 mL
1 1/2 cup	12 fl.oz.	355 mL
2 cups or 1 pint	16 fl.oz.	475 mL
4 cups or 1 quart	32 fl.oz.	1 L
1 gallon	128 fl.oz.	4 L

Temperatures Equivalents

FAHRENHEIT(F)	CELSIUS(C) APPROXIMATE)
225 °F	107 °C
250 °F	120 ° °C
275 °F	135 °C
300 °F	150 °C
325 °F	160 °C
350 °F	180 °C
375 °F	190 °C
400 °F	205 °C
425 °F	220 °C
450 °F	235 °C
475 °F	245 °C
500 °F	260 °C

Weight Equivalents

US STANDARD	METRIC (APPROXIMATE)
1 ounce	28 g
2 ounces	57 g
5 ounces	142 g
10 ounces	284 g
15 ounces	425 g
16 ounces (1 pound)	455 g
1.5 pounds	680 g
2 pounds	907 g

Air Fryer Cooking Chart

Food	Temperature (°C)	Cooking Time (minutes)
French fries (thin)	200	10-15
French fries (thick)	200	15-20
Chicken wings	180	20-25
Chicken breast	180	15-20
Salmon fillet	200	8-10
Shrimp	200	8-10
Onion rings	200	8-10
Vegetables (broccoli, etc.)	180	10-15
Frozen vegetables (mix)	180	10-15
Breaded fish fillets	200	10-12
Hamburgers	200	8-10
Bacon	180	6-8
Sausages	180	12-15
Meatballs	180	12-15
Baked potatoes	200	45-50
Sweet potatoes	200	20-25
Chicken breasts	200	15-20 min
Chicken thighs	200	20-25 min
Chicken wings	200	18-20 min
Fish fillets	200	8-12 min
Shrimp	200	6-8 min
Scallops	200	6-8 min
Salmon	200	10-12 min
Pork chops	200	12-15 min
Pork tenderloin	200	20-25 min
Steak (1 inch thick)	200	8-10 min
Hamburger patties	200	8-10 min
Hot dogs/sausages	200	6-8 min
French fries	200	15-20 min
Sweet potato fries	200	15-20 min
Potato wedges	200	15-20 min
Onion rings	200	12-15 min
Zucchini/squash fries	200	10-12 min
Broccoli/cauliflower	200	8-10 min
Brussel sprouts	200	12-15 min
Carrots	200	12-15 min
Asparagus	200	6-8 min

Food	Temperature (°C)	Cooking Time (minutes)
Corn on the cob	200	12-15 min
Baked potatoes	200	40-45 min
Stuffed mushrooms	200	8-10 min
Roasted peppers	200	8-10 min
Chicken nuggets	200	10-12 min
Meatballs	200	10-12 min
Spring rolls	200	10-12 min
Mozzarella sticks	200	6-8 min
Jalapeno poppers	200	8-10 min
Quiche	180	25-30 min
Puff pastry	200	10-12 min
Apple turnovers	200	12-15 min
Chocolate chip cookies	180	6-8 min

Note: Cooking times may vary depending on the type and brand of air fryer, as well as the size and thickness of the food being cooked. Always refer to the manufacturer's instructions and use a food thermometer to ensure that food is cooked to a safe temperature.

Chapter 3
English Breakfasts

Full English Breakfast (Metric)

Looking for a healthier way to enjoy a Full English Breakfast without sacrificing the classic flavors? Look no further! This Air Fryer Full English Breakfast recipe is the perfect way to start your day, with all the traditional breakfast favorites cooked to perfection in an air fryer with just a touch of cooking spray. Crispy bacon, juicy sausages, roasted tomatoes and mushrooms, tangy black pudding, and perfectly fried eggs - all packed with flavor and ready to be devoured in just a few minutes. Plus, with the air fryer, you'll get all the deliciousness without the added calories from deep frying. So, let's get cooking and start your day off right with this tasty and easy-to-make Air Fryer Full English Breakfast!

Prep time: 5 minutes | Cook time: 15 minutes| Serves 2

- 2 rashers of bacon (50g)
- 2 sausages (100g)
- 1 tomato, halved (100g)
- 1 cup of button mushrooms, sliced (100g)
- 2 large eggs
- 1 slice of black pudding (50g)
- Salt and pepper, to taste
- Cooking spray

1. Preheat your air fryer to 200°C.
2. Spray the air fryer basket with cooking spray.
3. Add the bacon and sausages to the basket, making sure they're not touching each other. Cook for 5 minutes.
4. After 5 minutes, add the halved tomato and sliced mushrooms to the basket. Sprinkle salt and pepper over the veggies. Cook for another 5 minutes.
5. Add the black pudding and cook for a further 2 minutes.
6. Crack the eggs into the basket, on the side of the other ingredients. Cook for 2-3 minutes, or until the whites are set and the yolks are still runny.
7. Remove the basket from the air fryer and serve the Full English Breakfast hot.
8. Enjoy your delicious and healthy Full English Breakfast, cooked to perfection in an air fryer!

Egg Sandwich (Metric)

Here's an air fryer recipe for an Egg Sandwich that you can make easily at home. This classic breakfast dish is perfect for a quick and satisfying morning meal or for any time of day when you're in the mood for a tasty sandwich. Using an air fryer for this recipe ensures that the bread is perfectly toasted and the egg is cooked to perfection. Plus, the recipe is easy to follow and can be customized to suit your taste preferences. Let's get started!

Prep time: 5 minutes | Cook time: 15 minutes| Serves 2

- 2 slices of bread
- 2 eggs
- 1 tbsp butter
- Salt and pepper to taste

1. Preheat the air fryer at 180°C for 5 minutes.
2. While the air fryer heats up, crack the eggs into a small bowl and beat them lightly. Add salt and pepper to taste.
3. Spread butter on both slices of bread.
4. Place the slices of bread into the air fryer basket.
5. Pour the beaten eggs on one slice of bread and spread it evenly.
6. Close the air fryer basket and cook for 5 minutes.
7. Remove the basket and put the slices of bread together, with the egg on top of the other slice.
8. Serve hot.
9. Enjoy your delicious air fryer Egg Sandwich!

Kippers Recipe (Metric)

Kippers are a classic British breakfast dish that consists of smoked herring, often served with toast or boiled potatoes. This recipe provides a quick and easy way to prepare kippers in an air fryer, resulting in a delicious and healthy breakfast option. The smoky flavor and tender texture of the fish, combined with a variety of herbs and spices, make for a tasty and satisfying meal to start the day.

Prep time: 5 minutes | Cook time: 10 minutes| Serves 2

- 2 fresh kippers
- 1 tablespoon olive oil
- Salt and pepper, to taste
- Lemon wedges, for serving

1. Preheat the air fryer to 180°C.
2. Rinse the kippers under cold water and pat them dry with paper towels.
3. Brush the kippers with olive oil on both sides and season with salt and pepper.
4. Place the kippers in the air fryer basket, skin-side down, and cook for 5-7 minutes or until the skin is crispy and the flesh is cooked through.
5. Remove the kippers from the air fryer and serve with lemon wedges.
6. Enjoy your delicious and healthy air fryer kippers!

English Scones (Metric)

English scones are a classic British tea-time treat that are perfect for a quick and easy breakfast or snack. These buttery and crumbly scones are often served with jam and clotted cream, and are best enjoyed with a cup of tea. This air fryer recipe for English scones is a modern twist on a traditional recipe and produces light and fluffy scones that are perfect for any occasion.

Prep time: 5 minutes | Cook time: 15 minutes| Serves 3

- 250g all-purpose flour
- 2 tsp baking powder
- 40g caster sugar
- 1/4 tsp salt
- 50g unsalted butter, chilled and cubed
- 120ml milk
- 1 egg, beaten
- Jam and clotted cream, to serve

1. Preheat the air fryer to 180°C (350°F).
2. In a large bowl, whisk together the flour, baking powder, sugar, and salt.
3. Add the chilled butter cubes and use your fingers to rub the butter into the flour mixture until it resembles coarse crumbs.
4. Add the milk and mix until just combined. Do not overmix.
5. Turn the dough out onto a floured surface and gently knead until it comes together. Flatten the dough to about 2cm thickness.
6. Use a 6cm round cookie cutter to cut out scones.
7. Brush the scones with the beaten egg.
8. Place the scones in the air fryer basket and cook for 8-10 minutes or until golden brown.
9. Serve the scones warm with jam and clotted cream.
10. Enjoy your delicious and easy-to-make Air Fryer English Scones!

English Tea And Toast (Metric)

English toast, also known as "eggs in a basket" or "toad in a hole," is a simple and delicious breakfast dish that can be prepared quickly and easily. The dish consists of a piece of bread with a hole cut out in the center, in which an egg is cracked and fried. It is a popular breakfast item in many households and can be enjoyed with a variety of toppings, such as bacon, cheese, or avocado. In this recipe, we will be using an air fryer to make this classic breakfast dish, resulting in a perfectly crispy and golden toast with a soft and runny egg center.Traditionally, the English eat their toast with butter and cheese. The toast pairs alongside black teas, such as English breakfast tea and Earl Grey.

However, other teas, such as green and herbal teas are becoming more popular with the English. This dish is the simplest to make at home and can be ready in minutes.

Prep time: 5 minutes | Cook time: 10 minutes| Serves 3

- 2 slices of bread
- 2 large eggs
- 2 tbsp butter
- Salt and pepper to taste

1. Preheat the air fryer to 180°C.
2. Use a biscuit cutter or the rim of a glass to cut a hole in the center of each slice of bread.
3. Spread butter on one side of each slice of bread and place them in the air fryer basket, buttered side down.
4. Crack an egg into each hole.
5. Season with salt and pepper to taste.
6. Air fry for 5-7 minutes, or until the egg is cooked to your liking.
7. Serve hot and enjoy your delicious English eggs in a basket!

Note: Cooking time may vary depending on the brand and model of your air fryer.

Eggy Bread (Metric)

Eggy bread, also known as French toast, is a classic breakfast dish that is simple and quick to make. It involves dipping slices of bread into an egg mixture and frying them until golden brown. It's a great way to use up leftover bread and perfect for a weekend brunch or a quick breakfast on the go. In this recipe, we'll be using an air fryer to create a healthier version of this beloved dish. The air fryer provides a crispy exterior without the need for frying in oil, making it a healthier and easier alternative.

Prep time: 5 minutes | Cook time: 10 minutes| Serves 3

- 2 large eggs
- 50ml whole milk
- 1/2 tsp vanilla extract
- 4 slices of bread
- 1 tbsp butter
- Maple syrup or jam for serving (optional)

1. Preheat the air fryer to 180°C.
2. In a mixing bowl, whisk together the eggs, milk, and vanilla extract until well combined.
3. Dip the bread slices into the egg mixture, making sure they are coated evenly.
4. Melt the butter in a frying pan over medium heat. Once melted, add the bread slices and cook for 2-3 minutes on each side until golden brown.
5. Transfer the cooked bread to the air fryer basket and cook for an additional 3-5 minutes, or until the bread is crispy and golden brown.
6. Serve hot with maple syrup or jam, if desired.
7. Enjoy your delicious Eggy Bread cooked to perfection in the air fryer!

English Crumpet Recipe (Metric)

English crumpets are a classic breakfast food in the UK, and they are perfect for a lazy weekend brunch. They are soft, fluffy, and have a slightly sour taste that pairs well with sweet or savory toppings. Traditionally, crumpets are cooked on a griddle or a stove, but this air fryer recipe will make the process even easier and quicker. Here is how to make delicious English crumpets in your air fryer.

Prep time: 15 minutes | Cook time: 55 minutes| Serves 4

- 200g all-purpose flour
- 1 teaspoon active dry yeast
- 1 teaspoon salt
- 1 teaspoon sugar
- 200ml warm milk
- 100ml warm water
- 1 teaspoon baking powder
- Butter, for spreading
- Jam or honey, for serving (optional)

1. In a mixing bowl, whisk together the flour, yeast, salt, and sugar.
2. Add the warm milk and warm water to the dry ingredients and mix until well combined.
3. Cover the mixing bowl with a towel and let the dough rise for 30-45 minutes in a warm place.
4. Preheat the air fryer to 180°C.
5. Stir in the baking powder into the dough.
6. Grease the air fryer basket with cooking spray or butter.
7. Spoon the dough into the greased air fryer basket, making sure to fill it up to about 2/3 of the way full.
8. Place the basket into the air fryer and cook for 7-10 minutes or until the crumpet is golden brown on the top.
9. Remove the crumpet from the air fryer and let it cool for a few minutes.
10. Use a fork to split the crumpet open, and then spread butter onto each half. Serve with jam or honey, if desired.
11. Enjoy your delicious and easy air fryer English crumpets!

Drop Scone (Metric)

Drop scones, also known as Scotch pancakes, are a traditional Scottish treat that make a great breakfast or snack. These small, fluffy pancakes are easy to make and perfect for serving with a variety of toppings, such as butter, jam, or syrup. In this recipe, we'll be using an air fryer to cook the drop scones, making them even easier and quicker to prepare.

Prep time: 5 minutes | Cook time: 10 minutes| Serves 3

- 120g self-raising flour
- 1 tbsp caster sugar
- 1 medium egg
- 75ml milk
- 1/2 tsp baking powder
- 1/2 tsp vanilla extract
- 1 pinch of salt
- Butter, for greasing

1. Preheat the air fryer to 180°C.
2. In a mixing bowl, sift the self-raising flour, baking powder, and salt together. Add the caster sugar and mix until well combined.
3. In another bowl, whisk the egg, milk, and vanilla extract together.
4. Gradually pour the wet ingredients into the dry ingredients while stirring constantly until a smooth batter forms.
5. Grease the air fryer basket with butter and drop spoonfuls of the batter onto the basket.
6. Cook the drop scones for 4-5 minutes until they are golden brown and slightly risen.
7. Serve the drop scones warm with your desired toppings such as honey, jam, or fresh berries.
8. Enjoy your delicious drop scones made in the air fryer!

Butteries Recipe (Metric)

Butteries, also known as rowies, are a traditional Scottish bread roll made with flour, lard, and butter. They have a crispy exterior and a soft, flaky interior that makes them perfect for breakfast or as a snack. In this recipe, we will be using an air fryer to make these delicious butteries with a healthier twist. With the use of an air fryer, the butteries will come out with a crispy exterior and soft and fluffy interior, without the need for deep-frying.

Prep time: 15 minutes | Cook time: 45 minutes| Serves 4

- 500g strong white flour
- 10g salt
- 10g caster sugar
- 10g fast-action dried yeast
- 60g lard
- 60g unsalted butter
- 250ml cold water
- 50g plain flour for dusting

1. In a mixing bowl, combine the strong white flour, salt, caster sugar, and fast-action dried yeast.
2. Add the lard and unsalted butter and mix until the mixture resembles breadcrumbs.
3. Gradually add the cold water and mix until a dough forms.
4. Knead the dough for 10 minutes until smooth and elastic.
5. Cover the dough with a tea towel and leave to rest for 30 minutes.
6. Preheat the air fryer to 160°C.
7. Divide the dough into 12 equal pieces and shape into circles.
8. Dust a clean surface with plain flour and place the circles of dough onto it.
9. Dust the tops of the dough circles with more flour.
10. Place the dough circles into the air fryer basket, making sure they are not touching.
11. Cook the butteries in the air fryer for 8-10 minutes or until golden brown.
12. Remove from the air fryer and leave to cool on a wire rack.
13. Serve warm with butter or jam, or fill them with your favourite sandwich fillings.
14. Enjoy your delicious homemade butteries!

Chapter 4
British National Treasures

Toad-In-The-Hole Recipe (Metric)

Toad-in-the-hole is a traditional British dish made with sausages baked in a batter that rises and forms a crispy outer layer. This hearty and comforting meal is perfect for any occasion and is a favorite among many households in the UK. This air fryer recipe puts a modern twist on the classic dish, making it quick and easy to prepare while maintaining the delicious flavors and textures that make it so beloved.

Prep time: 15 minutes | Cook time: 35 minutes| Serves 4

- 8 pork sausages
- 140g plain flour
- 2 eggs
- 175ml whole milk
- 2 tbsp sunflower oil
- Salt and pepper

1. Preheat the air fryer to 180°C.
2. Place the sausages in a single layer in the air fryer basket and cook for 5 minutes.
3. In a mixing bowl, whisk together the flour, eggs, and whole milk until smooth. Season with salt and pepper.
4. Once the sausages have cooked for 5 minutes, remove the air fryer basket and pour the batter over the sausages.
5. Return the air fryer basket to the air fryer and cook for a further 15-20 minutes until the batter has risen and turned golden brown.
6. Remove from the air fryer and serve hot with your choice of vegetables and gravy.
7. Enjoy your delicious and easy Air Fryer Toad-in-the-Hole!

Scotch Egg (Metric)

If you're looking for a tasty and easy-to-make snack or breakfast, look no further than these delicious Scotch Eggs! Made with sausage meat and boiled eggs, these crispy treats are perfect for on-the-go or as a party appetizer. With the help of your trusty air fryer, you can have them ready to enjoy in just 15 minutes. Plus, they're versatile enough to be served with your favourite dipping sauces, or simply enjoyed as is. Give this recipe a try and impress your friends and family with your culinary skills!

Prep time: 15 minutes | Cook time: 15 minutes| Makes 4 Scotch Eggs

- 4 large eggs
- 400g sausage meat
- 50g breadcrumbs
- 1 tbsp fresh parsley, chopped
- 1 tsp dried thyme
- 1 tsp dried rosemary
- 1 tsp smoked paprika
- Salt and pepper, to taste
- 50g plain flour
- 1 beaten egg
- 100g panko breadcrumbs
- Cooking oil spray

1. Preheat the air fryer to 200°C.
2. Place the eggs in a saucepan, cover with cold water, and bring to the boil. Once boiling, reduce heat to a simmer and cook for 6 minutes. Remove from the heat, drain the water, and immediately place the eggs in a bowl of ice water to cool.
3. In a mixing bowl, combine the sausage meat, breadcrumbs, parsley, thyme, rosemary, smoked paprika, salt, and pepper. Mix until well combined.
4. Divide the sausage meat mixture into 4 portions. Take one portion and flatten it out to form a disc. Place a boiled egg in the center of the disc and wrap the sausage meat around it, ensuring it is completely covered. Repeat for the remaining eggs.
5. Place the flour, beaten egg, and panko breadcrumbs into separate bowls. Roll each Scotch egg in flour, then dip into the beaten egg and finally roll in the panko breadcrumbs to coat.
6. Lightly spray the air fryer basket with cooking oil spray. Place the Scotch eggs in the basket and cook for 15 minutes, turning once, until golden brown and crispy.
7. Remove the Scotch eggs from the air fryer and allow them to cool for a few minutes before slicing in half and serving.
8. Enjoy your delicious and crispy Scotch Eggs, perfect for breakfast or as a snack!

Bangers And Mash Recipe (Metric)

Bangers and Mash is a classic British comfort food dish that consists of sausages and mashed potatoes, often served with onion gravy. This recipe gives a modern twist to the traditional dish by cooking the sausages and potatoes in an air fryer, resulting in a healthier and easier version that is just as delicious. The dish is perfect for a cozy night in or a casual dinner with friends and family.

Prep time: 15 minutes | Cook time: 25 minutes| Serves 4

- 4 large pork sausages
- 1 kg potatoes, peeled and chopped
- 50 g unsalted butter
- 1/2 cup whole milk
- Salt and black pepper, to taste
- 1 tablespoon olive oil
- 2 onions, sliced
- 2 cloves garlic, minced
- 2 tablespoons all-purpose flour
- 1 cup beef stock
- 2 teaspoons Worcestershire sauce
- 1 tablespoon fresh thyme leaves

1. Preheat the air fryer to 200°C.
2. In a large pot, add the chopped potatoes and cover with cold water. Bring to a boil over high heat, then reduce heat to medium-low and simmer for 15-20 minutes, or until the potatoes are soft.
3. Drain the potatoes and add the butter and milk. Mash until smooth and season with salt and black pepper.
4. While the potatoes are cooking, heat the olive oil in a large pan over medium heat. Add the sliced onions and minced garlic and sauté until the onions are soft and translucent.
5. Add the sausages to the pan and cook for 5-7 minutes, turning occasionally, until browned on all sides.
6. Sprinkle the flour over the sausages and onions, stirring to coat evenly. Cook for 1-2 minutes, then gradually pour in the beef stock, stirring constantly.
7. Add the Worcestershire sauce and thyme leaves, and bring to a simmer. Reduce heat to low and cook for 5-10 minutes, or until the gravy has thickened.
8. Transfer the sausage and onion mixture to the air fryer basket and cook for 8-10 minutes, or until the sausages are cooked through and golden brown.
9. Serve the bangers and mash hot with the thick gravy poured over the top. Enjoy!

British Fish And Chips (Metric)

Get ready for a classic British comfort food made healthier with the help of an air fryer! This recipe for fish and chips uses minimal oil and still produces crispy, golden fish fillets and chips that are just as delicious as the traditional deep-fried version. With a few simple ingredients and an air fryer, you can easily recreate this beloved dish in the comfort of your own home.

Prep time: 15 minutes | Cook time: 55 minutes| Serves 4

- 500g cod or haddock fillets, cut into 4-5 pieces
- 1 lemon, cut into wedges
- 500g potatoes, cut into thick chips
- 2 tbsp olive oil
- 1 tsp paprika
- 1 tsp garlic powder
- 1 tsp onion powder
- 1/2 tsp salt
- 1/4 tsp black pepper
- 50g plain flour
- 1 large egg, beaten
- 50g breadcrumbs

1. Preheat your air fryer to 200°C.
2. In a large bowl, toss the potatoes with olive oil, paprika, garlic powder, onion powder, salt, and pepper until well coated. Transfer to the air fryer basket and cook for 20 minutes, shaking the basket halfway through cooking time.
3. Meanwhile, season the fish fillets with salt and pepper. Place the flour, beaten egg, and breadcrumbs in separate bowls. Dredge each fish fillet in flour, shaking off any excess. Dip in the beaten egg, then coat in breadcrumbs.
4. Once the chips have cooked for 20 minutes, place the fish fillets in the air fryer basket and cook for 8-10 minutes or until golden brown and crispy, flipping halfway through cooking time.
5. Serve the fish and chips with lemon wedges on the side.
6. Enjoy your crispy and delicious British fish and chips made in the air fryer!

Classic Fish Fingers, Chips, And Beans (Metric)

Fish fingers, chips, and beans is a classic British dish that is beloved by both children and adults alike. This comforting meal is quick and easy to make, and it's perfect for a family dinner or a lazy weekend lunch. In this recipe, we'll be using an air fryer to cook the fish fingers and chips, which results in a healthier and less greasy version of this classic dish. With the addition of a can of baked beans, this meal is both satisfying and delicious.

Prep time: 15 minutes | Cook time: 25 minutes| Serves 4

- 4-6 frozen fish fingers
- 2 medium potatoes, cut into chips
- 1 tablespoon olive oil
- Salt and pepper
- 1 can of baked beans
- Optional: ketchup or tartar sauce, for serving

1. Preheat the air fryer to 200°C (400°F).
2. Toss the potato chips with olive oil, salt, and pepper.
3. Place the potato chips in the air fryer basket and cook for 10-12 minutes or until golden brown and crispy.
4. While the chips are cooking, place the frozen fish fingers in the air fryer basket and cook for 8-10 minutes or until cooked through and crispy.
5. While the chips and fish fingers are cooking, heat up the baked beans in a small saucepan or in the microwave.
6. Serve the fish fingers and chips with a side of baked beans and ketchup or tartar sauce, if desired.
7. Enjoy this classic British meal made healthier and easier with an air fryer!

Deep-Fried Onion Rings (Metric)

Deep-fried onion rings are a classic side dish that can be enjoyed on their own or alongside your favorite burger or sandwich. These crispy, golden-brown rings of sweet onion are perfect for any occasion, whether it's game day, a backyard barbecue, or a casual weeknight dinner. With the help of an air fryer, you can enjoy the same delicious flavor and texture of traditional deep-fried onion rings, but with less oil and fewer calories. In this recipe, we'll show you how to make perfectly crispy and flavorful onion rings using just a handful of ingredients and your trusty air fryer.

Prep time: 5 minutes | Cook time: 15 minutes| Serves 4

- 2 large onions, sliced into rings
- 1 cup all-purpose flour
- 1 teaspoon paprika
- 1 teaspoon garlic powder
- 1 teaspoon salt
- 1/2 teaspoon black pepper
- 1 cup breadcrumbs
- 2 eggs, beaten
- Cooking spray

1. Preheat the air fryer to 200°C (400°F).
2. In a large mixing bowl, combine the flour, paprika, garlic powder, salt, and black pepper.
3. Place the breadcrumbs in a separate bowl.
4. Dip each onion ring into the flour mixture, then into the beaten eggs, and finally into the breadcrumbs. Ensure that the onion rings are fully coated in each layer.
5. Place the onion rings into the air fryer basket in a single layer, ensuring that they are not touching.
6. Spray the onion rings with cooking spray to help them become crispy.
7. Air fry for 8-10 minutes, flipping the onion rings halfway through, until they are golden brown and crispy.
8. Serve immediately with your favorite dipping sauce.
9. Enjoy your delicious, crispy deep-fried onion rings made in the air fryer!

Spotted Dick Recipe (Metric)

Spotted Dick is a classic British dessert made with suet and dried fruit, traditionally steamed. But did you know you can make it in an air fryer? This recipe uses the air fryer to create a moist and fluffy sponge cake filled with delicious raisins and currants. Serve with a dollop of custard for the ultimate comfort dessert.

Prep time: 15 minutes | Cook time: 25 minutes| Serves 4

- 150g self-raising flour
- 75g shredded suet
- 75g caster sugar
- 75g mixed raisins and currants
- 1 egg
- 1 tbsp milk
- Custard, to serve

1. In a bowl, mix together the flour, shredded suet, caster sugar, and mixed raisins and currants.
2. In a separate bowl, beat the egg and milk together.
3. Add the egg mixture to the dry ingredients and mix until a soft dough forms.
4. Roll the dough into a cylinder shape, about 10cm long.
5. Place the cylinder into a heat-proof dish that will fit into the air fryer basket.
6. Cover the dish with foil, making sure there is space for the pudding to rise.
7. Preheat the air fryer to 160°C.
8. Place the dish in the air fryer basket and cook for 25-30 minutes, until the pudding is cooked through.
9. Remove from the air fryer and let rest for a few minutes before slicing.
10. Serve warm with custard.
11. Enjoy your delicious air fryer Spotted Dick!

Fish And Chips Recipe (Metric)

Fish and Chips is a classic British dish that has been enjoyed for generations. The dish consists of battered and fried fish served with crispy chips (French fries) and tartar sauce. This air fryer recipe provides a healthier take on the traditional recipe, without sacrificing any of the delicious flavors and textures. By using the air fryer, you can achieve perfectly crispy fish and chips without the need for deep-frying in oil.

Prep time: 15 minutes | Cook time: 25 minutes| Serves 4

- 4 large potatoes, peeled and sliced into thick chips
- 2 tablespoons olive oil
- Salt and pepper to taste
- 4 pieces of white fish fillets (haddock or cod)
- 1/2 cup all-purpose flour
- 1/2 teaspoon garlic powder
- 1/2 teaspoon paprika
- 1/4 teaspoon cayenne pepper (optional)
- 1 egg, beaten
- 1 cup panko breadcrumbs
- Lemon wedges, for serving
- Tartar sauce, for serving

1. Preheat your air fryer to 200°C.
2. Place the sliced potatoes in a large bowl and toss with olive oil, salt, and pepper.
3. Transfer the potatoes to the air fryer basket and cook for 15-20 minutes, shaking the basket occasionally, until the chips are golden brown and crispy.
4. While the chips are cooking, prepare the fish. In a shallow bowl, mix together the flour, garlic powder, paprika, and cayenne pepper (if using).
5. Dip the fish fillets in the beaten egg, then coat in the seasoned flour mixture.
6. Dip the fish fillets back into the egg mixture, then coat in the panko breadcrumbs, pressing the breadcrumbs onto the fish to ensure they stick.
7. Place the breaded fish fillets in the air fryer basket and cook for 8-10 minutes, or until the fish is cooked through and the breadcrumbs are crispy.
8. Serve the fish and chips with lemon wedges and tartar sauce.
9. Enjoy your delicious and healthier version of Fish and Chips made in the air fryer!

Beef Wellington Recipe (Metric)

Beef Wellington is a classic British dish that consists of beef tenderloin coated with a layer of mushroom duxelles, wrapped in puff pastry, and baked until golden brown. This elegant dish is perfect for special occasions and dinner parties. In this recipe, we will be using an air fryer to achieve a crispy, flaky crust while keeping the beef tender and juicy.

Prep time: 15 minutes | Cook time: 35 minutes| Serves 4

- 500g beef fillet
- Salt and pepper
- 2 tbsp olive oil
- 50g unsalted butter
- 1 large shallot, finely chopped
- 2 garlic cloves, minced
- 250g chestnut mushrooms, finely chopped
- 2 tbsp fresh thyme leaves
- 100ml dry white wine
- 320g puff pastry
- 1 egg yolk, beaten
- 1 tsp water

1. Preheat your air fryer to 200°C.
2. Season the beef fillet with salt and pepper. Heat olive oil in a frying pan over high heat, then sear the beef fillet until browned on all sides. Remove from heat and let it cool.
3. In the same pan, melt butter over medium heat. Add chopped shallot and garlic, and cook until softened. Add chopped mushrooms and fresh thyme leaves, and cook until the mushrooms release their moisture.
4. Pour in white wine and cook until it's reduced by half. Remove from heat and let it cool.
5. Roll out the puff pastry into a rectangle that's large enough to wrap around the beef fillet.
6. Spread the mushroom mixture onto the puff pastry, leaving a border around the edges.
7. Place the beef fillet on top of the mushroom mixture.
8. Use the puff pastry to wrap the beef fillet, sealing it tightly. Trim off any excess pastry.
9. Brush the beaten egg yolk and water mixture onto the puff pastry.
10. Place the beef Wellington in the air fryer and cook for 20-25 minutes or until the puff pastry is golden brown and crispy and the beef is cooked to your desired doneness.
11. Remove from the air fryer and let it rest for a few minutes before slicing and serving. Enjoy!

Chapter 5
Pies and Puddings

Cottage Pie (Metric)

This recipe is a quick and easy version of the classic British dish, Cottage Pie. Using an air fryer to cook the minced beef and mashed potato topping saves time and creates a delicious crispy texture. Packed with flavourful ingredients like Worcestershire sauce and thyme, this dish is sure to be a crowd-pleaser.

Prep time: 15 minutes | Cook time: 25 minutes| Serves 4

- 500g minced beef
- 2 tablespoons olive oil
- 1 onion, chopped
- 2 garlic cloves, minced
- 1 tablespoon tomato paste
- 1 tablespoon Worcestershire sauce
- 1 cup beef broth
- 2 cups mixed vegetables (carrots, peas, corn)
- 500g potatoes, peeled and cubed
- 2 tablespoons butter
- 1/4 cup milk
- Salt and pepper, to taste
- Chopped fresh parsley, for garnish

1. In a large skillet, heat olive oil over medium-high heat. Add onion and garlic and cook until softened, about 3-4 minutes. Add the minced beef and cook until browned, breaking it up into small pieces with a wooden spoon.
2. Stir in the tomato paste, Worcestershire sauce, and beef broth. Add the mixed vegetables and bring to a simmer. Let the mixture cook for 10-12 minutes, stirring occasionally, until the liquid has reduced and the mixture has thickened. Season with salt and pepper to taste.
3. In the meantime, place the cubed potatoes in a pot of boiling water and cook until tender, about 12-15 minutes. Drain and mash the potatoes with butter and milk until smooth.
4. Preheat the air fryer to 200°C.
5. Transfer the beef and vegetable mixture into an oven-safe dish. Spoon the mashed potatoes over the top, spreading it evenly. Place the dish in the air fryer basket and cook for 10-12 minutes or until the potatoes are golden brown and crispy.
6. Garnish with chopped parsley and serve hot.
7. Enjoy your delicious and savory Air Fryer Cottage Pie!

Shepherd's Pie (Metric)

This classic British dish is a hearty and satisfying meal that's perfect for any night of the week. Made with savory ground beef or lamb, vegetables, and a creamy mashed potato topping, this Shepherd's Pie is sure to become a family favorite. Plus, with the help of an air fryer, it's easy to make and requires minimal cleanup!

Prep time: 15 minutes | Cook time: 35 minutes| Serves 4

- For the filling:
- 500g ground beef or lamb
- 1 onion, chopped
- 2 carrots, peeled and diced
- 2 cloves garlic, minced
- 2 tbsp tomato paste
- 1 tsp dried thyme
- 1 tsp dried rosemary
- 1 cup beef or vegetable broth
- 2 tbsp flour
- 1 cup frozen peas
- Salt and pepper, to taste
- 1 kg potatoes, peeled and chopped into small pieces
- 1/4 cup milk
- 2 tbsp butter
- Salt and pepper, to taste
- 1 egg yolk

1. Preheat the air fryer to 200°C.
2. In a large skillet over medium-high heat, cook the ground beef or lamb until browned and cooked through, breaking up any clumps with a spoon.
3. Add the onion, carrots, and garlic to the skillet and cook until the vegetables are soft, about 5-7 minutes.
4. Stir in the tomato paste, thyme, and rosemary, and cook for another minute.
5. Sprinkle the flour over the mixture and stir until it's well combined.
6. Slowly pour in the broth, stirring constantly, and bring the mixture to a simmer.
7. Reduce the heat to medium-low and cook for another 5-7 minutes, or until the mixture has thickened.
8. Stir in the frozen peas and season the mixture with salt and pepper to taste.
9. In a separate pot, boil the potatoes until they are tender, then drain them and mash them with the milk, butter, salt, and pepper until they are smooth.
10. Beat the egg yolk and mix it into the mashed potatoes.
11. Spread the meat mixture evenly into a large baking dish or pie dish.
12. Spoon the mashed potatoes over the top of the meat mixture and smooth it out evenly.
13. Place the dish in the air fryer basket and cook for 10-15 minutes, or until the top of the pie is golden brown and crispy.
14. Serve hot and enjoy!
15. Note: You can customize this recipe by adding different vegetables, using a different type of ground meat, or using sweet potatoes instead of regular potatoes for the topping.

Steak And Ale Hand Pies (Metric)

Looking for a delicious and easy-to-make snack or lunch option? These Steak and Ale Hand Pies are perfect! The savory filling is packed with tender steak, earthy mushrooms, and rich ale, all wrapped up in a flaky pastry shell. And with the help of an air fryer, they're ready in no time at all. Serve them hot as a comforting meal or pack them up for a tasty on-the-go snack.

Prep time: 25 minutes | Cook time: 15 minutes| Makes 4 kit baking paper, rolling pin

- 1 tbsp vegetable oil
- 1 onion, diced
- 2 garlic cloves, minced
- 500g beef steak, cut into small pieces
- 1 tbsp plain flour
- 1 tbsp tomato paste
- 250ml ale
- 1 beef stock cube
- 1 tbsp Worcestershire sauce
- 1 tsp dried thyme
- Salt and pepper, to taste
- 320g puff pastry
- 1 egg, beaten

1. Preheat your air fryer to 200°C.
2. Heat the vegetable oil in a large frying pan over medium heat. Add the diced onion and minced garlic, and cook until softened.
3. Add the beef steak and cook until browned on all sides.
4. Stir in the flour and tomato paste, and cook for 1-2 minutes.
5. Add the ale, crumbled beef stock cube, Worcestershire sauce, dried thyme, salt, and pepper. Bring to a simmer and cook until the sauce has thickened and the beef is tender, about 10-15 minutes.
6. Remove the beef mixture from the heat and allow to cool slightly.
7. Roll out the puff pastry on a lightly floured surface to a thickness of about 3mm.
8. Cut the puff pastry into 4 equal squares. Place a spoonful of the beef mixture onto one half of each square, leaving a border around the edge.
9. Brush the edges of the pastry with beaten egg and fold the pastry over to enclose the filling. Crimp the edges with a fork to seal.
10. Place the hand pies onto a sheet of baking paper in the air fryer basket. Brush the tops of the pies with beaten egg.
11. Cook the hand pies in the air fryer at 200°C for 12-15 minutes, or until the pastry is golden brown and crispy.
12. Serve hot with a side salad or some vegetables. Enjoy!

British Apple Pie Recipe (Metric)

British apple pie is a classic dessert that has been enjoyed for generations. Made with sweet, juicy apples and a flaky pastry crust, it is a perfect dessert for any occasion. This air fryer recipe makes the process easier and quicker, resulting in a delicious apple pie with less fuss and mess.

Prep time: 15 minutes | Cook time: 20 minutes| Serves 4

- 500g apples, peeled and sliced
- 50g unsalted butter
- 50g light brown sugar
- 1 tsp ground cinnamon
- 1/2 tsp ground nutmeg
- 1/4 tsp ground cloves
- 1/4 tsp salt
- 1 tbsp cornstarch
- 1 tbsp lemon juice
- 1 sheet of ready-made shortcrust pastry
- 1 sheet of ready-made puff pastry
- 1 egg, beaten

1. Preheat the air fryer to 200°C.
2. In a saucepan, melt the butter and brown sugar together over medium heat.
3. Add the sliced apples, ground cinnamon, ground nutmeg, ground cloves, and salt. Stir well to combine.
4. In a small bowl, whisk together the cornstarch and lemon juice until smooth. Add it to the saucepan and stir until the mixture thickens, about 5 minutes.
5. Remove the saucepan from the heat and let the apple mixture cool.
6. Roll out the shortcrust pastry and line a greased 7-inch pie dish. Trim any excess pastry from the edges.
7. Spoon the cooled apple mixture into the pastry-lined pie dish.
8. Roll out the puff pastry and place it on top of the apple mixture. Trim any excess pastry from the edges.
9. Brush the beaten egg over the top of the puff pastry.
10. Place the pie dish in the air fryer and cook for 15 minutes or until the pastry is golden brown.
11. Remove the pie dish from the air fryer and let the pie cool for a few minutes before serving.
12. Enjoy your delicious air fryer British apple pie!

Steak And Kidney Pie Recipe (Metric)

Steak and kidney pie is a classic British dish that is hearty, comforting and delicious. It features tender chunks of beef and kidney in a rich and savory gravy, all encased in a flaky pastry crust. This air fryer version of the recipe is a quicker and healthier alternative to the traditional oven-baked version. With the help of the air fryer, you can achieve a perfectly cooked pie with a crisp, golden crust and a tender, flavorful filling. It's a perfect dish for a cozy dinner on a cold night.

Prep time: 15 minutes | Cook time: 35 minutes| Serves 4

- 500g beef steak, diced
- 250g lamb or beef kidney, trimmed and diced
- 2 tbsp plain flour
- 1 tbsp Worcestershire sauce
- 1 onion, diced
- 2 cloves garlic, minced
- 1 large carrot, peeled and diced
- 1 tbsp thyme leaves
- 250ml beef stock
- 1 sheet of pre-made puff pastry, thawed
- 1 egg, beaten
- Salt and black pepper, to taste
- Olive oil spray

1. Preheat the air fryer to 180°C.
2. In a large bowl, toss the diced beef and kidney in the plain flour until evenly coated. Season with salt and black pepper.
3. Spray the air fryer basket with olive oil spray and add the diced beef and kidney. Cook for 5-6 minutes or until browned on all sides. Transfer to a plate and set aside.
4. In the same air fryer basket, add the diced onion, minced garlic, and diced carrot. Cook for 2-3 minutes or until softened.
5. Add the thyme leaves, tomato puree, and Worcestershire sauce to the basket and stir to combine.
6. Return the cooked beef and kidney to the basket and pour in the beef stock. Stir well to combine.
7. Cook for 5-6 minutes or until the mixture has thickened slightly. Remove from the air fryer and let it cool slightly.
8. Roll out the puff pastry on a lightly floured surface and cut a circle slightly larger than the size of the air fryer basket.
9. Transfer the beef and kidney mixture to a greased baking dish that fits inside the air fryer basket. Lay the pastry circle over the top and press the edges down to seal.
10. Brush the beaten egg over the top of the pastry.
11. Place the baking dish into the air fryer basket and cook for 12-15 minutes or until the pastry is golden brown and puffed up.
12. Serve the steak and kidney pie hot with your favourite sides.
13. Enjoy your delicious steak and kidney pie made in the air fryer!

Fish Pie Recipe (Metric)

Fish pie is a classic comfort food that is perfect for a cozy night in. This creamy and delicious dish is typically made with a variety of fish, potatoes, and a rich sauce. While traditionally cooked in the oven, this recipe will show you how to make a tasty fish pie using an air fryer, making it a quick and easy meal that's sure to satisfy.

Prep time: 15 minutes | Cook time: 35 minutes| Serves 4

- 500g fish fillets (such as haddock, cod, or salmon), cut into bite-size pieces
- 500g potatoes, peeled and cut into chunks
- 1 onion, chopped
- 2 cloves garlic, minced
- 1 tbsp butter
- 1 tbsp plain flour
- 250ml milk
- 1 tbsp chopped fresh parsley
- 1 tbsp chopped fresh dill
- 1 tbsp lemon juice
- Salt and pepper, to taste
- 50g grated cheddar cheese

1. Preheat the air fryer to 200°C (390°F).
2. Boil the potatoes until tender. Drain and mash with a bit of butter and milk until smooth. Set aside.
3. In a large saucepan, melt the butter over medium heat. Add the onion and garlic and sauté until softened.
4. Add the flour and stir until well combined with the butter and onion mixture.
5. Gradually pour in the milk, whisking constantly to avoid lumps.
6. Continue to whisk until the mixture thickens.
7. Add the fish pieces, parsley, dill, lemon juice, salt, and pepper to the saucepan. Stir until the fish is coated in the sauce.
8. Pour the fish and sauce mixture into an oven-safe dish.
9. Spread the mashed potatoes over the fish and sauce, making sure to cover the entire surface.
10. Sprinkle grated cheese on top.
11. Place the dish in the air fryer and cook for 15-20 minutes until the cheese is melted and the potatoes are golden brown.
12. Serve hot and enjoy!
13. Note: You can add other vegetables such as peas, carrots, or corn to the fish pie mixture if desired.
14. Enjoy your delicious and easy-to-make air fryer fish pie!

Scottish Mealy Pudding (Metric)

This air fryer recipe is a delicious and easy way to make Scottish Mealy Pudding. Made with oatmeal, onions, and beef suet, this traditional Scottish delicacy is a hearty and flavorful addition to any meal. Using the air fryer allows you to cook the pudding quickly and evenly, resulting in a crispy outer layer and a soft, moist center. Serve it as a side dish or as part of a Scottish-inspired feast.

Prep time: 15 minutes | Cook time: 25 minutes | Serves 4

- 300g Scottish mealy pudding, sliced
- 1 tablespoon vegetable oil
- Salt and pepper to taste
- Optional: Brown sauce or HP sauce for serving

1. Preheat the air fryer to 180°C.
2. Lightly brush the sliced mealy pudding with vegetable oil.
3. Place the mealy pudding slices in the air fryer basket in a single layer, making sure they don't overlap.
4. Cook for 10 minutes, then flip the slices over and cook for an additional 10 minutes or until crispy and golden brown.
5. Remove from the air fryer and season with salt and pepper to taste.
6. Serve hot with brown sauce or HP sauce on the side, if desired.
7. Note: Cooking time may vary depending on the size and power of your air fryer. Adjust the cooking time accordingly and check the mealy pudding slices regularly to prevent burning.

Scottish White Pudding (Metric)

Here's a recipe for Scottish White Pudding cooked in an air fryer. Scottish white pudding is a traditional Scottish sausage made from pork, oats, and spices. This recipe is easy to follow and uses the air fryer to cook the pudding to perfection. Enjoy this classic Scottish delicacy as part of your breakfast or any meal of the day.

Prep time: 15 minutes | Cook time: 15 minutes | Serves 4

- 200g Scottish white pudding, sliced into rounds
- 1 tbsp vegetable oil

1. Preheat your air fryer to 200°C.
2. Lightly brush or spray the air fryer basket with vegetable oil to prevent sticking.
3. Arrange the white pudding rounds in a single layer in the air fryer basket.
4. Cook for 5-7 minutes, flipping the rounds halfway through the cooking time, until the pudding is golden brown and crispy.
5. Serve hot with your favorite breakfast items or as a snack.
6. Note: Cooking time may vary depending on the thickness of the white pudding rounds and the power of your air fryer. Check the pudding regularly to avoid overcooking.

Basic English Pudding (Metric)

This basic pudding recipe is a classic British dessert that is perfect for a cozy winter evening. The warm and rich pudding is made with simple ingredients that are easily found in your pantry, and the steaming process creates a moist and tender texture that is hard to resist. Serve it with your favorite custard or sauce for a satisfying and comforting dessert that will surely impress your family and friends.

Prep time: 15 minutes | Cook time: 2 hours 25 minutes| Serves 4

- 125g self-raising flour
- 125g suet
- 125g caster sugar
- 2 eggs
- 1 tsp vanilla extract
- 100g raisins
- 100g currants
- 50g chopped dates
- 1 tsp mixed spice
- Milk, as needed

1. In a large mixing bowl, combine the self-raising flour, suet, and caster sugar.
2. Add the eggs and vanilla extract, and mix well to combine.
3. Stir in the raisins, currants, chopped dates, and mixed spice.
4. Add enough milk to create a soft, dropping consistency. The amount of milk needed may vary, so add it gradually until the mixture is the right consistency.
5. Grease a pudding basin with butter, and pour in the pudding mixture.
6. Cover the basin with a piece of greased baking paper, then a piece of aluminium foil. Tie securely with string to create a watertight seal.
7. Place the basin in the air fryer basket, and pour in enough boiling water to come halfway up the sides of the basin.
8. Cook at 160°C for 2 to 2 1/2 hours, until the pudding is cooked through and a skewer inserted into the centre comes out clean.
9. Remove the pudding from the air fryer and let it cool for a few minutes before turning it out onto a serving dish.
10. Serve hot with custard, cream, or your favourite pudding sauce.
11. Note: Steamed puddings can also be made ahead of time and reheated in the air fryer. Simply wrap the cooled pudding in foil and store in the fridge for up to 2 days. When ready to serve, reheat in the air fryer at 160°C for 15-20 minutes.

Bread And Butter Pudding Recipe (Metric)

Bread and Butter Pudding is a classic British dessert that is loved by many. This pudding is made by layering slices of buttered bread with raisins and custard, and then baked until golden and crispy on top. It's the perfect comfort food for cold winter nights, and can be served with a dollop of whipped cream or a scoop of ice cream for added indulgence. In this recipe, we'll show you how to make a delicious Bread and Butter Pudding in an air fryer, using metric measurements.

Prep time: 15 minutes | Cook time: 25 minutes| Serves 4

- 6 slices of bread, preferably stale
- 50g unsalted butter, softened
- 50g raisins or sultanas
- 2 medium eggs
- 150ml whole milk
- 50g caster sugar
- 1 tsp vanilla extract
- 1/2 tsp ground cinnamon
- Pinch of salt

1. Preheat the air fryer to 160°C (320°F).
2. Spread the softened butter on one side of each bread slice.
3. Cut the bread slices into quarters.
4. Arrange the bread pieces in the air fryer basket, buttered-side up, and sprinkle the raisins or sultanas over the top.
5. In a separate bowl, whisk together the eggs, milk, sugar, vanilla extract, ground cinnamon, and a pinch of salt until well combined.
6. Pour the egg mixture over the bread and raisins in the air fryer basket.
7. Air fry the bread and butter pudding for 15-20 minutes, or until the top is golden brown and the custard is set.
8. Serve the bread and butter pudding warm with custard, cream or ice cream, if desired.
9. Enjoy your delicious bread and butter pudding cooked to perfection in an air fryer!

Sticky Toffee Pudding (Metric)

Sticky Toffee Pudding is a classic British dessert that is perfect for any occasion. This rich and decadent pudding is made with dates and covered in a sweet toffee sauce that is sure to satisfy any sweet tooth. This air fryer recipe is a quick and easy way to make this delicious dessert with a fluffy texture and a crispy edge. It's the perfect comfort food to enjoy on a cozy night in with loved ones.

Prep time: 15 minutes | Cook time: 35 minutes| Serves 4

- 200g pitted dates, chopped
- 250ml boiling water
- 1 tsp bicarbonate of soda
- 75g unsalted butter, softened
- 175g caster sugar
- 2 eggs
- 175g self-raising flour
- 1 tsp vanilla extract
- 150g dark brown sugar
- 150ml double cream
- 50g unsalted butter

1. Preheat the air fryer to 180°C.
2. Grease a round cake tin that fits in the air fryer.
3. Put the chopped dates in a bowl and pour the boiling water over them. Add the bicarbonate of soda and let the mixture cool for 10 minutes.
4. In a separate bowl, cream together the softened butter and caster sugar until light and fluffy.
5. Add the eggs one at a time, beating well after each addition.
6. Sift in the self-raising flour and fold it into the mixture.
7. Stir in the cooled date mixture and vanilla extract until well combined.
8. Pour the mixture into the prepared cake tin and smooth the surface.
9. Place the cake tin in the air fryer basket and cook for 20-25 minutes or until a skewer inserted into the centre of the cake comes out clean.
10. While the cake is cooking, make the toffee sauce. In a small saucepan, combine the dark brown sugar, double cream, and unsalted butter. Cook over medium heat, stirring constantly, until the sugar has dissolved and the mixture has thickened slightly.
11. Remove the cake from the air fryer and allow it to cool for a few minutes.
12. Serve the cake warm with the toffee sauce spooned over the top. Enjoy!

Note: The cooking time may vary depending on the size and type of air fryer you're using. Adjust accordingly.

Rice Pudding Recipe (Metric)

Rice pudding is a classic comfort food that has been enjoyed for centuries. This creamy and sweet dessert is simple to make and uses basic pantry staples, making it a perfect choice for a cozy evening at home. With this air fryer recipe, you can enjoy the rich, comforting flavors of rice pudding without having to spend hours cooking it on the stovetop. The air fryer method also allows for a perfect balance of creaminess and texture that will leave you wanting more.

Prep time: 15 minutes | Cook time: 25 minutes| Serves 4

- 1/2 cup short-grain rice
- 2 cups milk
- 1/4 cup sugar
- 1/4 tsp salt
- 1 tsp vanilla extract
- 1/4 tsp ground cinnamon
- 1/4 cup raisins (optional)

1. Rinse the rice in cold water and drain it.
2. In a mixing bowl, combine the rice, milk, sugar, and salt, and mix well.
3. Add the vanilla extract and cinnamon, and mix until well combined.
4. Pour the mixture into a baking dish or oven-safe bowl that fits into the air fryer basket.
5. Optional: add raisins to the mixture and mix well.
6. Place the baking dish into the air fryer basket and cook at 320°F for 20 minutes.
7. Remove the baking dish from the air fryer and let it cool for a few minutes before serving.
8. Enjoy your delicious and creamy air fryer rice pudding!

Chapter 6
Meats

Chicken Tikka Masala (Metric)

Chicken Tikka Masala is a popular Indian dish made with marinated chicken cooked in a creamy and flavorful tomato-based sauce. It is a delicious and comforting dish that can be enjoyed with rice, naan bread, or other Indian side dishes. This air fryer recipe is a healthier twist on the classic dish, using less oil and cooking the chicken in an air fryer for a crispy texture.

Prep time: 15 minutes | Cook time: 25 minutes| Serves 4

- 500g boneless, skinless chicken breasts, cut into bite-sized pieces
- 1 cup plain yogurt
- 2 tablespoons lemon juice
- 2 teaspoons ground cumin
- 2 teaspoons paprika
- 1 teaspoon ground ginger
- 1 teaspoon ground cinnamon
- 1 teaspoon ground coriander
- 1/2 teaspoon cayenne pepper
- Salt and pepper, to taste
- 1 tablespoon olive oil
- 1 onion, finely chopped
- 4 garlic cloves, minced
- 1 tablespoon grated fresh ginger
- 1 red chili, finely chopped
- 1 tablespoon tomato paste
- 1 can (400g) chopped tomatoes
- 1/2 cup chicken stock
- 1/2 cup heavy cream
- Fresh cilantro, chopped, for serving

1. In a large bowl, mix together the yogurt, lemon juice, cumin, paprika, ground ginger, cinnamon, coriander, cayenne pepper, salt, and pepper.
2. Add the chicken pieces to the bowl, making sure they are coated evenly with the yogurt mixture. Cover and marinate in the refrigerator for at least 1 hour, or overnight.
3. Preheat the air fryer to 200°C.
4. Add the marinated chicken to the air fryer basket and cook for 10-12 minutes, or until the chicken is cooked through and browned.
5. In a separate pan, heat the olive oil over medium heat. Add the chopped onion and cook until translucent.
6. Add the garlic, fresh ginger, and red chili to the pan and cook for an additional 2-3 minutes, stirring frequently.
7. Stir in the tomato paste, chopped tomatoes, chicken stock, and heavy cream. Simmer for 5-10 minutes, or until the sauce has thickened.
8. Serve the chicken tikka masala with the sauce, and garnish with chopped cilantro. Enjoy with naan bread or rice.
9. Note: You can adjust the amount of cayenne pepper to your preference to make the dish more or less spicy.

Cumberland Sausage (Metric)

Cumberland sausage is a popular traditional sausage from the North West of England, known for its distinctive spiciness and coiled shape. This recipe is a healthier twist on the classic Cumberland sausage, made in an air fryer rather than frying in oil. The result is a juicy, flavorful sausage with a crispy exterior that is perfect for breakfast, lunch, or dinner.

Prep time: 15 minutes | Cook time: 20 minutes| Serves 4

- 4 Cumberland sausages
- 1 tablespoon olive oil
- Salt and pepper, to taste

1. Preheat the air fryer to 180°C (350°F).
2. Brush the sausages with olive oil and season with salt and pepper.
3. Place the sausages in the air fryer basket, leaving some space between each sausage.
4. Cook for 12-15 minutes, flipping the sausages halfway through, until they are cooked through and browned on the outside.
5. Remove from the air fryer and let them cool for a minute or two.
6. Serve hot with your favorite sides.
7. Enjoy your delicious air fryer Cumberland sausages!

Lamb Chops With Mint Sauce (Metric)

Roast Lamb with Mint Sauce is a classic British dish that is perfect for a special occasion or a cozy family dinner. The tender, juicy lamb is seasoned with herbs and spices, then cooked to perfection in the air fryer. The dish is served with a tangy and refreshing mint sauce that perfectly complements the rich flavors of the lamb. This recipe is easy to follow and will have you savoring every bite of this delicious dish in no time!

Prep time: 15 minutes | Cook time: 20 minutes| Serves 4

- 4 lamb chops
- 1 tbsp olive oil
- Salt and pepper to taste
- 1/4 cup chopped fresh mint leaves
- 2 tbsp white wine vinegar
- 2 tbsp honey
- 2 tbsp water

1. Preheat the air fryer to 400°F (200°C).
2. Rub the lamb chops with olive oil and season with salt and pepper.
3. Place the lamb chops in the air fryer basket and cook for 8-10 minutes, flipping halfway through.
4. While the lamb chops are cooking, make the mint sauce by combining the chopped mint leaves, white wine vinegar, honey, and water in a small bowl.
5. Serve the lamb chops with the mint sauce on the side.

Roast Dinner (Metric)

Air fryers are a great way to cook roast dinners quickly and easily. This recipe uses an air fryer to cook roast beef, potatoes, carrots, and Yorkshire pudding to perfection. The result is a delicious and satisfying meal that can be enjoyed any day of the week. Here is a recipe for a roast dinner in the air fryer using the metric measurement:

Prep time: 15 minutes | Cook time: 45 minutes| Serves 4

- 500g beef roast
- 500g potatoes
- 2 tbsp olive oil
- Salt and pepper
- 1 cup beef broth
- 1/4 cup red wine
- 1 tbsp cornstarch
- 1 tbsp water
- 1 packet of Yorkshire pudding mix
- 2 eggs
- 120ml milk

1. Preheat the air fryer to 180°C.
2. Season the beef roast with salt and pepper.
3. In a bowl, toss the potatoes, carrots, chopped onion, and minced garlic with olive oil and season with salt and pepper.

4. Place the beef roast and vegetables in the air fryer basket and cook for 20 minutes.
5. Remove the basket and flip the beef roast and vegetables. Cook for another 20 minutes.
6. In a small saucepan, heat the beef broth and red wine over medium heat.
7. In a separate bowl, mix the cornstarch and water together to create a slurry.
8. Once the beef roast and vegetables are cooked, remove them from the air fryer basket and set aside.
9. Add the slurry to the beef broth and wine mixture and whisk until the mixture thickens. Set aside.
10. In a bowl, mix together the Yorkshire pudding mix, eggs, and milk until combined.
11. Pour the Yorkshire pudding mixture into the air fryer basket and cook for 15 minutes or until golden brown.
12. Serve the beef roast, vegetables, and Yorkshire pudding with the beef gravy on the side. Enjoy!

Gammon Steak, Egg, And Chips (Metric)

Gamon steak, egg, and chips is a classic British pub dish that is popular for its simplicity and hearty flavor. This dish consists of a thick cut of gammon steak, which is a type of cured ham, served with a fried egg and crispy chips (fries). It's a perfect comfort food that is easy to prepare and satisfying to eat. In this recipe, we'll show you how to cook gammon steak, egg, and chips using an air fryer, which will give you the same delicious result as traditional deep frying but with less oil and hassle.

Prep time: 15 minutes | Cook time: 45 minutes| Serves 4

- 2 gammon steaks (approximately 200g each)
- 2 large potatoes, peeled and cut into chips
- 1 tablespoon olive oil
- Salt and pepper
- 2 large eggs
- Fresh parsley (optional)

1. Preheat the air fryer to 200°C.
2. Place the gammon steaks in the air fryer basket and cook for 8-10 minutes, flipping halfway through, until they are cooked to your desired doneness.
3. While the gammon steaks are cooking, toss the potato chips in olive oil and season with salt and pepper.
4. When the gammon steaks are done, remove them from the air fryer basket and cover them with foil to keep them warm.
5. Add the seasoned potato chips to the air fryer basket and cook for 15-20 minutes, shaking the basket occasionally, until they are crispy and golden brown.
6. In a separate pan, fry two eggs to your desired doneness.
7. Serve the gammon steaks, chips, and eggs on a plate, garnished with fresh parsley if desired.
8. Enjoy your gammon steak, egg, and chips, made easily and quickly in your air fryer!

Sunday Roast (Metric)

Air fryer Sunday roast is a quick and easy way to enjoy a traditional British meal with minimal effort. This classic Sunday roast recipe features a succulent roast chicken, crispy roast potatoes, tender roasted carrots, and fluffy Yorkshire pudding. Using an air fryer to cook this meal cuts down on cooking time and reduces the need for multiple pots and pans, making it a convenient and fuss-free option for a delicious family dinner. Here's the recipe with metric measurements:

Prep time: 15 minutes | Cook time: 55 minutes| Serves 4

- 1 whole chicken (around 1.5 kg)
- 800g potatoes, peeled and cut into chunks
- 4 carrots, peeled and cut into chunks
- 2 tbsp olive oil
- 1 tsp dried rosemary
- Salt and black pepper, to taste
- 200g plain flour
- 3 eggs
- 300ml milk
- 1 tsp vegetable oil

1. Preheat your air fryer to 180°C.
2. Season the chicken with salt, black pepper, and dried rosemary, then place it in the air fryer basket and cook for 40 minutes.
3. Meanwhile, toss the potatoes and carrots in olive oil and season with salt and black pepper.
4. After the chicken has cooked for 40 minutes, add the potatoes and carrots to the air fryer basket and continue cooking for another 20 minutes.
5. While the chicken and vegetables are cooking, prepare the Yorkshire pudding batter. Whisk together the flour, eggs, milk, and vegetable oil until smooth.
6. Pour the batter into a greased baking dish or muffin tin, then place it in the air fryer basket with the chicken and vegetables for the last 10 minutes of cooking.
7. Once the chicken is cooked through and the vegetables and Yorkshire pudding are crispy and golden, remove everything from the air fryer and serve hot. Enjoy your delicious Sunday roast!

Sausage Roll Recipe (Metric)

Sausage rolls are a classic British snack that can be enjoyed at any time of the day. They are perfect for picnics, parties, or as a quick and easy snack. This air fryer recipe for sausage rolls is easy to make and takes less time than the traditional oven-baked recipe. The sausage rolls come out crispy on the outside and juicy on the inside, making them a delicious treat for any occasion.

Prep time: 15 minutes | Cook time: 25 minutes| Serves 4

- 375g puff pastry
- 500g sausage meat
- 1 egg, beaten
- 1 tbsp. milk
- Salt and pepper to taste
- Optional: sesame seeds or poppy seeds

1. Preheat your air fryer to 180°C (356°F).
2. Roll out the puff pastry into a large rectangle, roughly 30cm x 20cm.
3. Spread the sausage meat evenly over the pastry, leaving a small border around the edges.
4. Roll up the pastry tightly around the sausage meat, making sure to seal the edges with a little bit of water.
5. Cut the roll into small sausage rolls, around 10-12cm in length.
6. Brush the tops of the sausage rolls with the beaten egg and milk mixture.
7. Sprinkle with sesame seeds or poppy seeds, if desired.
8. Place the sausage rolls in the air fryer basket, making sure to leave a little bit of space between them.
9. Air fry for 12-15 minutes, until golden brown and cooked through.
10. Serve hot with your favorite dipping sauce. Enjoy!

British Steak Slices (Metric)

This recipe for British Steak Slices is perfect for a quick and easy weeknight dinner. Tender slices of beef are coated in a delicious seasoning and cooked to perfection in the air fryer. The result is a deliciously crispy and flavorful dish that your whole family will love. Enjoy these steak slices on their own, or pair them with your favorite sides for a complete meal.

Prep time: 15 minutes | Cook time: 25 minutes | Serves 4

- 4 beef steak slices (150g each)
- 2 tablespoons olive oil
- 1 onion, diced
- 2 cloves garlic, minced
- 2 tablespoons tomato paste
- 1 teaspoon Worcestershire sauce
- 1 teaspoon dried thyme
- 1 teaspoon dried rosemary
- 1 teaspoon paprika
- 1 teaspoon salt
- 1/2 teaspoon black pepper
- 500g puff pastry
- 1 egg, beaten

1. Preheat your air fryer to 200°C.
2. Heat the olive oil in a frying pan over medium heat. Add the onion and garlic, and cook until the onion is soft and translucent.
3. Add the tomato paste, Worcestershire sauce, thyme, rosemary, paprika, salt, and pepper. Stir until well combined.
4. Add the beef slices to the pan and cook for 2-3 minutes on each side until browned.
5. Roll out the puff pastry on a floured surface and cut into four equal-sized pieces.
6. Place a beef slice on each piece of pastry and top with the onion mixture.
7. Brush the edges of the pastry with beaten egg and fold over to encase the beef and onion mixture.
8. Brush the top of each steak slice with beaten egg.
9. Place the steak slices into the air fryer basket, leaving space between them.
10. Cook for 15-20 minutes or until the pastry is golden brown and the beef is cooked to your liking.
11. Serve with your favourite sides.
12. Enjoy your delicious air fryer British steak slices!

Balti (Metric)

Balti is a spicy Pakistani-style curry that originated in Birmingham, England. This flavorful dish is a popular choice in many Indian and Pakistani restaurants across the world. Traditionally, balti is cooked in a balti pan, a type of wok-shaped cooking vessel. In this recipe, we'll show you how to make a delicious and authentic balti using an air fryer and metric measurements. The dish is perfect for a cozy night in or for entertaining friends and family. So, let's get started!

Prep time: 15 minutes | Cook time: 25 minutes | Serves 4

- 500g boneless, skinless chicken breasts, diced
- 2 tbsp Balti curry paste
- 1 onion, finely chopped
- 1 green pepper, deseeded and chopped
- 400g canned chopped tomatoes
- 2 garlic cloves, crushed
- 1 tsp ground cumin
- 1 tsp ground coriander
- 1 tsp garam masala
- 2 tbsp vegetable oil
- 100ml chicken stock
- Salt and pepper, to taste
- Chopped fresh coriander, to garnish

1. Preheat your air fryer to 180°C (350°F).
2. In a bowl, mix the chicken with the Balti curry paste and set aside.
3. In a separate bowl, mix together the chopped onion, green pepper, canned chopped tomatoes, crushed garlic, ground cumin, ground coriander, and garam masala.
4. Add the vegetable oil to a frying pan and heat it over medium-high heat.
5. Once the oil is hot, add the chicken and cook for 3-4 minutes until it has browned.
6. Add the onion and pepper mixture to the frying pan and stir everything together.
7. Pour in the chicken stock and season with salt and pepper.
8. Transfer everything to your air fryer basket and cook for 15-20 minutes, stirring occasionally.
9. Once cooked, remove the Balti from the air fryer and serve hot, garnished with chopped fresh coriander.
10. Enjoy your homemade air fryer Balti!

Pork Pie Recipe (Metric)

Pork pie is a classic British dish that is often served as a snack or as part of a meal. It typically consists of a hot water crust pastry filled with seasoned pork and baked until golden and crispy. In this recipe, we'll be using an air fryer to cook the pork pies, resulting in a crunchy crust and juicy filling.

Prep time: 15 minutes | Cook time: 25 minutes| Serves 4

- 250g plain flour
- 75g lard
- 75g butter
- 1/2 tsp salt
- 1 egg, beaten
- 400g pork mince
- 1 small onion, finely chopped
- 1 garlic clove, minced
- 1 tsp dried thyme
- 1 tsp dried sage
- 1 tsp Worcestershire sauce
- Salt and pepper, to taste
- 1 egg, beaten (for egg wash)

1. Preheat your air fryer to 180°C.
2. In a mixing bowl, combine the plain flour and salt. Add in the lard and butter, and mix until the mixture resembles breadcrumbs.
3. Add in the beaten egg and mix until the dough comes together. If the mixture is too dry, add a little cold water.
4. Roll out the dough to a thickness of about 3mm. Cut out 6 circles using a round cutter or a glass.
5. Grease 6 individual pie tins with oil or butter, then carefully line each tin with a pastry circle.
6. In a mixing bowl, combine the pork mince, onion, garlic, thyme, sage, Worcestershire sauce, salt and pepper.
7. Divide the pork mixture equally among the 6 pastry cases.
8. Brush the edges of the pastry with beaten egg, then top each pie with another pastry circle.
9. Crimp the edges of the pastry together with a fork, and brush the top of each pie with beaten egg.
10. Place the pies into the air fryer basket and cook for 20-25 minutes, or until the pastry is golden brown and the filling is cooked through.
11. Remove the pies from the air fryer and let them cool for a few minutes before serving. Enjoy!

Cod Fish And Chips (Metric)

Air fryer cod fish and chips is a healthier and easier way to enjoy this classic British dish at home. The air fryer produces crispy fish and chips without the need for deep frying, making it a great option for those who want to indulge in this comfort food without the added oil and calories. Here's an air fryer recipe for cod fish and chips using the metric measurement:

Prep time: 15 minutes | Cook time: 15 minutes| Serves 4

- 500g cod fillets
- 200g all-purpose flour
- 1 tsp baking powder
- 1 tsp salt
- 250ml cold sparkling water
- 4 large potatoes, peeled and cut into fries
- 2 tbsp olive oil
- Salt and pepper, to taste
- Lemon wedges, to serve

1. Preheat the air fryer to 200°C.
2. In a large bowl, whisk together the flour, baking powder, and salt.
3. Slowly add the cold sparkling water to the flour mixture, whisking until the batter is smooth.
4. Dip each piece of cod into the batter, shaking off any excess, and place it into the air fryer basket.
5. In a separate bowl, toss the potato fries with olive oil, salt, and pepper until coated.
6. Add the potato fries to the air fryer basket, making sure they are spread out evenly.
7. Cook for 10-12 minutes or until the fish is golden brown and the potatoes are crispy, shaking the basket halfway through to ensure even cooking.
8. Serve hot with lemon wedges on the side. Enjoy!

Haddock Fish And Chips Recipe (Metric)

Air fryers are a great way to cook up crispy fish and chips without all the excess oil and mess that comes with deep frying. This recipe features haddock, a flaky and tender white fish, coated in a crispy breadcrumb crust and served alongside crispy chips. Using the air fryer to cook the fish and chips results in a delicious and healthier version of this classic British dish.

Prep time: 15 minutes | Cook time: 25 minutes| Serves 2

- 2 medium-sized haddock fillets, skinless
- 1/2 cup all-purpose flour
- 1/2 tsp garlic powder
- 1/2 tsp paprika
- 1/2 tsp salt
- 1/4 tsp black pepper
- 1 egg, beaten
- 1/2 cup breadcrumbs
- Cooking spray
- 2 medium-sized potatoes, cut into chips
- Salt, to taste

1. Preheat the air fryer to 200°C/400°F.
2. In a shallow dish, mix together the flour, garlic powder, paprika, salt, and black pepper.
3. Dip the haddock fillets in the flour mixture, shaking off any excess.
4. Dip the fillets into the beaten egg, then coat in the breadcrumbs.
5. Spray the air fryer basket with cooking spray.
6. Place the breaded haddock fillets into the air fryer basket and spray the tops with cooking spray.
7. Add the potato chips to the air fryer basket and season with salt to taste.
8. Cook for 12-15 minutes, flipping the fish and stirring the chips halfway through the cooking time, until the fish is golden brown and cooked through and the chips are crispy.
9. Serve the haddock fillets with the chips and your favorite dipping sauce. Enjoy!

Meat And Potato Pie (Metric)

Air fryers are a great way to cook savory pies and this recipe for meat and potato pie is no exception. Packed with tender chunks of beef and flavorful potatoes, this classic British comfort food is sure to please. The air fryer gives the pastry a perfectly crispy texture while keeping the filling juicy and delicious. Follow this easy recipe using metric measurements and you'll have a hearty and satisfying meal in no time.

Prep time: 15 minutes | Cook time: 45 minutes| Serves 4

- 500g beef chuck, cut into small chunks
- 2 large potatoes, peeled and diced
- 1 onion, chopped
- 2 garlic cloves, minced
- 2 tbsp tomato paste
- 2 cups beef broth
- 1 tsp Worcestershire sauce
- 1 tsp dried thyme
- Salt and pepper to taste
- 1 sheet puff pastry, thawed
- 1 egg, beaten

1. Preheat your air fryer to 180°C.
2. In a large bowl, season the beef with salt and pepper.
3. Heat a large skillet over medium-high heat and brown the beef on all sides. Remove and set aside.
4. In the same skillet, sauté the onion and garlic until translucent. Add the diced potatoes and cook for 2-3 minutes until slightly browned.
5. Stir in the tomato paste, beef broth, Worcestershire sauce, and thyme. Bring to a simmer and cook for 10-15 minutes or until the potatoes are tender.
6. Add the browned beef to the skillet and stir to combine.
7. Roll out the puff pastry and use it to line a 9-inch pie dish. Fill the dish with the beef and potato mixture.
8. Cut another sheet of puff pastry to fit on top of the filling. Brush the edges of the bottom pastry with the beaten egg and place the top pastry over the filling. Press the edges together to seal.
9. Brush the top of the pastry with the beaten egg and make a few small slits in the center to allow steam to escape.
10. Place the pie dish in the air fryer and cook for 20-25 minutes or until the pastry is golden brown and crispy.
11. Let the pie cool for a few minutes before slicing and serving. Enjoy!

Chapter 7
Vegetables

Bubble And Squeak (Metric)

Bubble and squeak is a classic British dish made from leftover vegetables, usually from a Sunday roast. The name comes from the sound the ingredients make as they cook in the pan. This dish is perfect for a quick and easy meal and can be served as a main dish or as a side dish to accompany a range of meat dishes. In this air fryer recipe, we will be using the metric measurement for the ingredients.

Prep time: 15 minutes | Cook time: 35 minutes| Serves 4

- 500g potatoes, peeled and chopped
- 300g mixed leftover vegetables, such as cabbage, Brussels sprouts, carrots, and peas
- 1 onion, diced
- 2 garlic cloves, minced
- 1 tablespoon olive oil
- Salt and pepper, to taste
- 4 large eggs

1. Preheat your air fryer to 180°C.
2. Boil the potatoes in a large pot of salted water for 15-20 minutes, until tender. Drain and set aside.
3. In a large frying pan, heat the olive oil over medium heat. Add the diced onion and minced garlic, and cook for 2-3 minutes until softened.
4. Add the leftover vegetables to the pan and cook for another 3-4 minutes until heated through.
5. Add the boiled potatoes to the pan and mash everything together with a fork or potato masher. Season with salt and pepper to taste.
6. Divide the mixture into 4 equal portions and shape them into patties.
7. Place the patties in the air fryer basket and cook for 10-12 minutes, flipping halfway through, until crispy and golden brown.
8. In the meantime, fry the eggs in a separate pan to your desired doneness.
9. Serve the bubble and squeak patties with the fried eggs on top.
10. Enjoy your delicious and easy air fryer bubble and squeak!

Rumbledethumps (Metric)

Rumbledethumps is a traditional Scottish dish that originated in the Scottish Borders region. It's a simple yet delicious dish that consists of mashed potatoes, cabbage, and onions baked together with cheese on top. Here's an air fryer version of the recipe that's easy to make and perfect for a cozy dinner.

Prep time: 15 minutes | Cook time: 25 minutes| Serves 4

- 500g potatoes, peeled and chopped
- 500g cabbage, shredded
- 1 onion, chopped
- 2 garlic cloves, minced
- 100g cheddar cheese, grated
- 2 tbsp butter
- Salt and pepper, to taste

1. Place the chopped potatoes in a pot of salted water and bring to a boil. Cook for 15-20 minutes, or until the potatoes are soft and tender.
2. In a separate pan, melt the butter and sauté the onions and garlic until they're soft and translucent. Add the shredded cabbage and continue to cook until it's wilted and tender.
3. Drain the potatoes and mash them with a potato masher or fork until smooth. Add the cabbage and onion mixture to the potatoes and stir well to combine. Season with salt and pepper to taste.
4. Preheat your air fryer to 180°C.
5. Grease a baking dish or air fryer-safe container and transfer the potato and cabbage mixture into it. Spread the grated cheddar cheese on top of the mixture.
6. Place the dish or container into the air fryer basket and cook for 10-15 minutes, or until the cheese is melted and bubbly and the dish is heated through.
7. Serve hot and enjoy your delicious air fryer Rumbledethumps!

Suet Dumplings (Metric)

Air fryers are not typically used for making suet dumplings, which are traditionally cooked in a stew or pot roast. However, it is possible to make suet dumplings in an air fryer for a delicious and crispy alternative. Here's a recipe for suet dumplings using the metric measurement:

Prep time: 5 minutes | Cook time: 15 minutes| Serves 4

- 200g self-raising flour
- 100g shredded suet
- 1 tsp dried mixed herbs
- 1/2 tsp salt
- 120ml water

1. In a mixing bowl, combine the self-raising flour, shredded suet, dried mixed herbs, and salt.
2. Add the water gradually and mix until you have a soft dough.
3. Roll the dough into small balls, around 2-3cm in diameter.
4. Preheat your air fryer to 180°C.
5. Place the dumplings in the air fryer basket, leaving some space in between.
6. Air fry the dumplings for 10-12 minutes until golden brown and crispy on the outside.
7. Serve immediately with your favourite stew or pot roast.
8. Enjoy your delicious and crispy suet dumplings made in the air fryer!

Cheesy Potato And Lentil Pie (Metric)

Air fryers can be used to make a variety of dishes, including savory pies. This cheesy potato and lentil pie is a hearty and filling vegetarian meal that is easy to make in an air fryer. The combination of tender lentils, creamy potatoes, and melted cheese makes for a delicious and satisfying dish. Here's the recipe using metric measurements:

Prep time: 15 minutes | Cook time: 25 minutes| Serves 4

- 500g potatoes, peeled and chopped
- 150g dried lentils, rinsed and drained
- 1 onion, chopped
- 2 cloves garlic, minced
- 1 tbsp olive oil
- 1 tsp dried thyme
- 1 tsp dried rosemary
- 200g cheddar cheese, grated
- Salt and pepper, to taste

1. Preheat your air fryer to 200°C.
2. In a large bowl, mix together the chopped potatoes, lentils, onion, garlic, olive oil, thyme, and rosemary. Season with salt and pepper.
3. Transfer the mixture to a baking dish that fits in your air fryer basket.
4. Cover the dish with foil and place it in the air fryer basket.
5. Cook for 20 minutes, then remove the foil and sprinkle the grated cheese on top.
6. Return the dish to the air fryer and cook for another 5-10 minutes, or until the cheese is melted and bubbly.
7. Serve hot and enjoy!

Vegetable Toad In The Hole (Metric)

Air fryers are a great way to make delicious and healthy meals, and this recipe for vegetable toad in the hole is no exception. This classic British dish features a hearty batter that is baked with a variety of vegetables, creating a filling and satisfying meal. By using an air fryer, you can achieve a crispy crust without the need for excess oil, making it a healthier option. This recipe serves 4 and uses the metric measurement.

Prep time: 15 minutes | Cook time: 35 minutes| Serves 4

- 200g plain flour
- 4 large eggs
- 250ml milk
- 1 tsp Dijon mustard
- 1/2 tsp salt
- 1/4 tsp black pepper
- 2 tbsp olive oil
- 2 red onions, sliced
- 2 red peppers, sliced
- 2 courgettes, sliced
- 2 garlic cloves, minced
- 1 tbsp fresh thyme leaves

1. Preheat the air fryer to 180°C.
2. In a large bowl, whisk together the flour, eggs, milk, mustard, salt and pepper until you have a smooth batter.
3. Heat the olive oil in a large frying pan over medium heat. Add the onions, peppers and courgettes and cook for 5-7 minutes, stirring occasionally, until the vegetables are tender and lightly browned. Stir in the garlic and thyme and cook for another minute.
4. Pour the batter over the vegetables in the frying pan and transfer to the air fryer basket.
5. Cook for 20-25 minutes or until the batter is golden brown and cooked through.
6. Serve the vegetable toad in the hole hot, garnished with additional thyme leaves if desired.

Baked Bean Pizza Recipe (Metric)

Looking for a quick and easy meal that's sure to satisfy your pizza cravings? Try this delicious and simple air fryer baked bean pizza recipe! The combination of baked beans and cheese on a crispy crust is sure to be a hit with both kids and adults alike.

Prep time: 15 minutes | Cook time: 15 minutes| Serves 4

- 1 pre-made pizza crust (thin or thick)
- 1 can of baked beans (400g)
- 1/2 cup of shredded cheddar cheese (60g)
- 1/2 cup of shredded mozzarella cheese (60g)
- 1/4 cup of diced onions (30g)
- 1/4 cup of diced bell peppers (30g)
- 1/4 cup of sliced mushrooms (30g)
- 1 tsp of olive oil (5ml)
- Salt and pepper, to taste
- Optional toppings: sliced tomatoes, chopped fresh herbs

1. Preheat your air fryer to 400°F (200°C).
2. Brush the pre-made pizza crust with olive oil.
3. Spread the baked beans over the pizza crust, leaving a small border around the edges.
4. Sprinkle the shredded cheddar cheese and mozzarella cheese over the baked beans.
5. Add the diced onions, bell peppers, and mushrooms on top of the cheese.
6. Season with salt and pepper, to taste.
7. Place the pizza in the air fryer basket and cook for 8-10 minutes, or until the crust is golden brown and the cheese is melted and bubbly.
8. Once cooked, remove the pizza from the air fryer basket and let it cool for a few minutes before slicing.
9. Optional: top with sliced tomatoes and chopped fresh herbs before serving.
10. Enjoy your delicious and easy air fryer baked bean pizza!

Glamorgan Sausages Recipe (Metric)

Glamorgan sausages are a traditional Welsh vegetarian dish made with cheese and leeks. They are usually coated in breadcrumbs and fried, but with the air fryer, you can achieve the same crispy texture with less oil. This recipe is easy to make and perfect for a vegetarian main course or a snack.

Prep time: 15 minutes | Cook time: 25 minutes| Serves 4

- 200g leeks, finely sliced
- 1 tbsp butter
- 150g breadcrumbs
- 150g Caerphilly cheese, grated
- 2 tbsp fresh parsley, chopped
- 1 tsp English mustard
- 1 tsp smoked paprika
- 1 egg, beaten
- Salt and pepper to taste
- Olive oil spray

1. In a frying pan, melt the butter over medium heat. Add the sliced leeks and cook until softened, around 5 minutes. Set aside to cool.
2. In a large mixing bowl, combine the breadcrumbs, grated cheese, chopped parsley, mustard, smoked paprika, salt, and pepper. Mix well.
3. Add the cooled leeks and beaten egg to the mixing bowl. Mix everything together until you have a sticky dough.
4. Divide the dough into 8-10 equal portions and shape each portion into a sausage shape. Place them onto a plate and refrigerate for 30 minutes to firm up.
5. Preheat the air fryer to 200°C (400°F) for 5 minutes.
6. Spray the sausages with olive oil spray and place them into the air fryer basket. Cook for 10-12 minutes, flipping the sausages halfway through, until golden brown and crispy on the outside.
7. Serve immediately, garnished with extra chopped parsley, if desired. These sausages are delicious on their own, but you can also serve them with a side of your choice, such as a green salad or roasted vegetables. Enjoy!

Vegetarian Shepherd's Pie (Metric)

Air fryers are a versatile appliance that can be used to make a variety of dishes, including vegetarian shepherd's pie. This recipe uses wholesome ingredients like lentils, vegetables, and mashed potatoes to create a comforting and satisfying meal. The air fryer helps to cook the vegetables and lentils evenly, while the mashed potatoes get a crispy top layer, making this vegetarian shepherd's pie both healthy and delicious.

Prep time: 15 minutes | Cook time: 35 minutes| Serves 4

- 1 large potato, peeled and chopped
- 1 large sweet potato, peeled and chopped
- 2 tablespoons olive oil
- 1 onion, chopped
- 2 garlic cloves, minced
- 1 carrot, chopped
- 1 celery stick, chopped
- 1/2 cup green lentils, rinsed and drained
- 1/2 cup vegetable stock
- 1/2 teaspoon dried thyme
- Salt and pepper, to taste
- 1/2 cup grated cheddar cheese
- 1 tablespoon chopped fresh parsley

1. Preheat the air fryer to 180°C.
2. In a large bowl, toss the chopped potatoes and sweet potatoes with 1 tablespoon of olive oil and season with salt and pepper. Place them in the air fryer basket and cook for 10-12 minutes or until they are tender.
3. Meanwhile, heat the remaining tablespoon of olive oil in a large pan over medium heat. Add the onion, garlic, carrot, and celery and cook for 5-6 minutes, until the vegetables are soft.
4. Add the lentils, vegetable stock, thyme, salt, and pepper to the pan and bring the mixture to a boil. Reduce the heat and simmer for 15-20 minutes, until the lentils are tender.
5. Once the potatoes are done, mash them with a fork or potato masher until they are smooth.
6. In a baking dish, spread the lentil mixture evenly on the bottom. Spread the mashed potatoes on top of the lentils, making sure to cover them completely.
7. Sprinkle the grated cheddar cheese on top of the mashed potatoes.
8. Place the baking dish in the air fryer basket and cook for 8-10 minutes, until the cheese is melted and bubbly.
9. Sprinkle chopped parsley on top of the Vegetarian Shepherd's Pie and serve hot. Enjoy!

Crispy Baked Tofu 'Chicken' Nuggets (Metric)

Air fryers are perfect for making delicious and healthy versions of classic dishes, and these crispy baked tofu 'chicken' nuggets are no exception. They're easy to make, packed with protein, and have a satisfying crunch that will keep you coming back for more. In this recipe, we'll be using firm tofu as a substitute for chicken, and coating it with a savory and crispy breading before air frying to perfection. Here's how to make crispy baked tofu 'chicken' nuggets in your air fryer using the metric measurement.

Prep time: 15 minutes | Cook time: 15 minutes| Serves 4

- 400g firm tofu
- 60g all-purpose flour
- 1 tsp paprika
- 1 tsp garlic powder
- 1 tsp onion powder
- 1/2 tsp salt
- 1/4 tsp black pepper
- 1 egg
- 100g breadcrumbs
- Cooking spray

1. Drain and press the tofu to remove excess water, then cut into bite-sized nuggets.
2. In a bowl, mix together the flour, paprika, garlic powder, onion powder, salt, and black pepper.
3. In another bowl, beat the egg.
4. Place the breadcrumbs in a third bowl.
5. Dip each tofu nugget in the flour mixture, then the egg, and finally coat in the breadcrumbs.
6. Place the coated nuggets in the air fryer basket and spray with cooking spray.
7. Air fry at 200°C for 10-12 minutes or until crispy and golden brown.
8. Serve hot with your favorite dipping sauce. Enjoy!

Chapter 8
Breads, Pastries And Biscuits

Cornish Pasty (Metric)

If you're looking for a classic Cornish treat that's easy to make in your air fryer, look no further than this Cornish Pasty recipe! Filled with a delicious mixture of beef, potatoes, and veggies, these handheld pies are perfect for a quick lunch or snack. Plus, cooking them in the air fryer gives them a perfectly crisp and flaky crust that's sure to satisfy.

Prep time: 25 minutes | Cook time:30 minutes| Makes 4 pasties

- 300g plain flour
- 150g butter, cubed
- 1 tsp salt
- 150ml cold water
- 200g beef skirt, finely diced
- 1 onion, finely diced
- 2 medium potatoes, peeled and diced
- 100g swede, peeled and diced
- Salt and pepper to taste
- 1 egg, beaten

1. In a large mixing bowl, combine the flour, salt and cubed butter. Rub the butter into the flour until it resembles breadcrumbs.
2. Gradually add in the cold water and mix until a smooth dough forms. Cover the bowl with cling film and let it rest for 30 minutes.
3. Preheat your air fryer to 200°C.
4. In another bowl, mix together the beef, onion, potatoes, and swede. Season with salt and pepper.
5. Divide the pastry dough into 4 equal pieces and roll them out into circles about 20cm in diameter.
6. Place a quarter of the filling mixture onto one side of each circle of pastry.
7. Brush the edges of the pastry with beaten egg and then fold the other half of the pastry over the filling. Pinch the edges together to seal.
8. Brush the tops of the pasties with beaten egg and then place them in the air fryer basket.
9. Air fry the pasties at 200°C for 10 minutes, then reduce the temperature to 160°C and cook for a further 20 minutes until the pasties are golden brown.
10. Serve hot or cold, as desired.
11. Enjoy your delicious Cornish pasties made in an air fryer!

Honey Buns Recipe (Metric)

Honey buns are a delicious treat that can be enjoyed any time of day. Whether you want a sweet snack or a breakfast pastry, these buns are sure to satisfy your cravings. Made with honey and cinnamon, these buns have a warm, comforting flavor that is perfect for cool autumn or winter days. In this air fryer recipe, you'll learn how to make honey buns quickly and easily, using the metric measurement.

Prep time: 15 minutes | Cook time: 25 minutes| Serves 4

- 350g all-purpose flour
- 2 tsp baking powder
- 1/4 tsp baking soda
- 1/4 tsp salt
- 60g unsalted butter, chilled and cut into small pieces
- 100ml buttermilk
- 60ml honey
- 1 large egg
- 1 tsp vanilla extract
- For the glaze:
- 60ml honey
- 30g unsalted butter
- 1/4 tsp vanilla extract
- A pinch of salt

1. Preheat your air fryer to 180°C.
2. In a large mixing bowl, combine the flour, baking powder, baking soda, and salt. Add the chilled butter and use a pastry cutter or your fingers to rub it into the flour mixture until the mixture resembles coarse crumbs.
3. In another bowl, whisk together the buttermilk, honey, egg, and vanilla extract.
4. Add the wet ingredients to the dry ingredients and stir until just combined.
5. Turn the dough out onto a lightly floured surface and knead it gently for a minute or two until it comes together.
6. Divide the dough into 8 equal pieces and shape each into a ball. Place the balls into the air fryer basket, leaving a little space between them.
7. Air fry the honey buns for 10-12 minutes or until they are golden brown and a toothpick inserted into the center comes out clean.
8. While the honey buns are cooking, make the glaze by melting the honey, butter, vanilla extract, and salt together in a small saucepan over medium heat.
9. Brush the honey buns with the glaze as soon as they come out of the air fryer. Serve warm.
10. Enjoy your delicious air fryer honey buns!

Plum Bread (Metric)

Plum bread is a traditional British fruit bread that is perfect for breakfast or as an afternoon snack. This recipe is easy to make in an air fryer, resulting in a moist and flavorful bread with a crispy crust. The addition of dried plums and mixed spice gives it a rich and delicious flavor, making it a great treat to enjoy with a cup of tea or coffee.

Prep time: 15 minutes | Cook time: 25 minutes| Serves 4

- 200g self-raising flour
- 1 tsp ground cinnamon
- 1/2 tsp ground ginger
- 1/4 tsp ground cloves
- 100g caster sugar
- 2 eggs
- 75g unsalted butter, melted
- 150g chopped dried plums
- 50g chopped walnuts
- 100ml milk

1. Preheat the air fryer to 160°C.
2. In a mixing bowl, whisk together the self-raising flour, cinnamon, ginger, cloves, and caster sugar.
3. In a separate bowl, beat the eggs and add in the melted butter.
4. Mix the chopped dried plums and walnuts into the dry ingredients.
5. Gradually stir the egg mixture into the dry ingredients until well combined.
6. Add the milk to the mixture and stir until smooth.
7. Grease a 7-inch cake tin and pour in the mixture.
8. Allow to cool before slicing and serving.
9. Enjoy your delicious Plum Bread made in an air fryer!

Welsh Rarebit (Metric)

Welsh rarebit, also known as Welsh rabbit, is a classic British dish that consists of a cheese sauce typically served on toasted bread. Despite its name, the dish does not actually contain any rabbit. This rich and savory dish is perfect for a hearty breakfast, lunch, or dinner. In this recipe, we will show you how to make a delicious Welsh rarebit in the air fryer using metric measurements.

Prep time: 5 minutes | Cook time: 15 minutes| Serves 4

- 4 slices of bread
- 50g butter
- 50g plain flour
- 200ml milk
- 100g grated cheddar cheese
- 1 tsp Dijon mustard
- 1 egg yolk
- Salt and pepper to taste

1. Preheat the air fryer to 200°C.
2. In a saucepan, melt the butter over medium heat.
3. Add the flour and whisk until combined. Cook for 1-2 minutes, stirring constantly.
4. Slowly pour in the milk while whisking. Continue to cook and whisk until the mixture has thickened.
5. Add the grated cheese and mustard and stir until the cheese has melted and the mixture is smooth.
6. Remove the pan from the heat and season with salt and pepper to taste.
7. Toast the bread slices in the air fryer for 1-2 minutes on each side.
8. Spoon the cheese mixture over the toast and return to the air fryer. Cook for 2-3 minutes, until the cheese is melted and bubbly.
9. Serve immediately.
10. Enjoy your delicious Welsh rarebit made in the air fryer!

Ginger Snap Biscuits (Metric)

Ginger snap biscuits, also known as ginger snaps, are a classic treat with a spicy kick. These crunchy biscuits are perfect for dipping in tea or enjoying on their own as a snack. In this air fryer recipe, we'll show you how to make these delicious biscuits with the added convenience of using an air fryer. The result is a perfectly crisp and flavorful ginger snap biscuit that will satisfy your sweet tooth.

Prep time: 5 minutes | Cook time: 15 minutes| Serves 4

- 200g all-purpose flour
- 1 tsp baking powder
- 1/2 tsp ground cinnamon
- 1/2 tsp ground ginger
- 1/4 tsp ground cloves
- 1/4 tsp salt
- 115g unsalted butter, at room temperature
- 100g granulated sugar
- 1 large egg
- 1 tbsp molasses
- 1/2 tsp vanilla extract

1. Preheat the air fryer to 160°C (320°F).
2. In a medium bowl, whisk together the flour, baking powder, cinnamon, ginger, cloves, and salt.
3. In a separate large bowl, cream the butter and sugar together until light and fluffy.
4. Beat in the egg, molasses, and vanilla extract until smooth.
5. Gradually mix in the dry ingredients until a dough forms.
6. Using your hands, shape the dough into small balls (about 1 inch in diameter) and place them on a greased air fryer basket.
7. Flatten the balls slightly with a fork.
8. Air fry for 8-10 minutes or until golden brown.
9. Allow the biscuits to cool for a few minutes before transferring them to a wire rack to cool completely.
10. Store in an airtight container at room temperature for up to 1 week.
11. Enjoy your delicious and crispy ginger snap biscuits made in an air fryer!

Eton Mess Recipe (Metric)

Eton Mess is a classic British dessert made with a combination of whipped cream, meringue, and fresh berries. It's a deliciously light and fluffy dessert that's perfect for a summertime treat or a special occasion. This recipe adds a twist to the traditional version by using an air fryer to quickly and easily make the meringue. The result is a dessert that's both sweet and tangy, with a delicate crunch from the meringue.

Prep time: 15 minutes | Cook time: 15 minutes| Serves 4

- 200g strawberries, hulled and sliced
- 150g raspberries
- 150g blueberries
- 100g caster sugar
- 200ml double cream
- 2 tbsp icing sugar
- 4 meringue nests, crushed

1. Preheat the air fryer to 180°C.
2. In a mixing bowl, combine the strawberries, raspberries, blueberries, and caster sugar.
3. Place the berry mixture in the air fryer basket and air fry for 10 minutes, stirring halfway through.
4. Meanwhile, in another bowl, whip the double cream and icing sugar until soft peaks form.
5. Once the berries are done, transfer them to a bowl and let them cool for a few minutes.
6. Add the crushed meringue nests to the bowl and stir gently to combine.
7. Fold in the whipped cream mixture.
8. Serve the Eton mess immediately and enjoy!

Baked Somerset Brie Recipe (Metric)

Baked Somerset Brie is a delicious and indulgent way to enjoy this creamy, rich cheese. This recipe takes it to the next level by using an air fryer to create a perfectly melted, gooey center with a crispy outer layer. Serve it as an appetizer or snack at your next gathering and watch as it disappears in minutes!

Prep time: 15 minutes | Cook time: 15 minutes| Serves 4

- 250g Somerset Brie cheese
- 1 clove of garlic, minced
- 1 tbsp. fresh thyme leaves
- 2 tbsp. honey
- 1/4 cup chopped walnuts
- 1 baguette, sliced

1. Preheat the air fryer to 180°C.
2. Remove the Somerset Brie from the packaging and place it in a small oven-safe dish.
3. Score the top of the cheese with a sharp knife.
4. Sprinkle minced garlic and fresh thyme leaves over the top of the cheese.
5. Drizzle honey over the cheese and sprinkle the chopped walnuts on top.
6. Place the dish with the cheese in the air fryer basket and cook for 6-8 minutes or until the cheese is melted and bubbly.
7. Serve with slices of baguette.
8. Enjoy your deliciously melted and gooey Baked Somerset Brie, perfect as an appetizer or snack!

Trifle Recipe (Metric)

Trifle is a classic British dessert that is perfect for any occasion. Layers of sponge cake, custard, jelly, and whipped cream come together to create a delightful and visually appealing dessert. This air fryer recipe puts a new spin on the traditional trifle, allowing you to create a delicious and impressive dessert with minimal effort. With the help of your air fryer, you can have a scrumptious trifle in no time!

Prep time: 15 minutes | Cook time: 15 minutes| Serves 4

- 250g sponge cake, cut into small cubes
- 400g mixed fruit, fresh or canned (berries, peaches, and pineapple work well)
- 1-2 tbsp sherry or fruit juice
- 400g custard, homemade or store-bought
- 200g whipped cream
- 50g chopped nuts (optional)
- Fresh fruit or berries, to decorate

1. Preheat the air fryer to 180°C.
2. Arrange the sponge cake cubes in the air fryer basket and cook for 5-6 minutes, until golden brown and crisp. Set aside to cool.
3. If using canned fruit, drain well. Otherwise, wash and prepare fresh fruit.
4. In a small bowl, mix the sherry or fruit juice with 2 tbsp of water. Brush the sponge cake cubes with the mixture.
5. In a trifle bowl or individual glasses, layer the sponge cake cubes, mixed fruit, and custard.
6. Top with whipped cream and sprinkle with chopped nuts (if using).
7. Chill in the fridge for at least an hour before serving.
8. Decorate with fresh fruit or berries before serving.
9. Enjoy this delicious and easy-to-make trifle in your air fryer!

Jam Roly Poly Recipe (Metric)

Jam Roly Poly is a classic British dessert made from a soft sponge dough rolled up with a generous spread of jam, then steamed or baked until golden brown. Served hot with custard or cream, it's a comforting and indulgent treat perfect for any occasion. In this air fryer recipe, we will show you how to make a delicious and easy version of Jam Roly Poly using the metric measurement, with a crisp and fluffy texture that will impress your guests.

Prep time: 15 minutes | Cook time: 35 minutes| Serves 4

- 250g self-raising flour
- 125g shredded suet
- 75g caster sugar
- 1/2 tsp salt
- 6 tbsp raspberry jam
- 125ml milk
- 1 egg, beaten
- 1 tsp vanilla extract
- Custard, to serve

1. Preheat the air fryer to 180°C (356°F).
2. In a large mixing bowl, combine the self-raising flour, shredded suet, caster sugar and salt.
3. In a separate bowl, mix together the milk, egg and vanilla extract.
4. Add the wet ingredients to the dry ingredients and mix until it forms a dough.
5. On a floured surface, roll out the dough into a rectangle about 0.5cm thick.
6. Spread the raspberry jam over the dough, leaving a small border around the edge.
7. Roll up the dough tightly from one of the long edges and seal the seam by pinching the dough together.
8. Place the rolled dough onto a sheet of baking paper and then onto the air fryer basket. Cook for 25-30 minutes or until golden brown and cooked through.
9. Allow the jam roly poly to cool slightly before slicing into rounds and serving with custard.
10. Enjoy your delicious and easy air fryer jam roly poly!

Cornish Fairings Recipe (Metric)

Cornish Fairings are a traditional spicy ginger biscuit that originated in Cornwall, England. They are a favorite of locals and tourists alike and are often enjoyed with a cup of tea or coffee. This air fryer recipe provides a quick and easy way to make these delicious biscuits at home, with the added benefit of being healthier than the traditional deep-fried version.

Prep time: 15 minutes | Cook time: 15 minutes| Serves 4

- 200g plain flour
- 100g caster sugar
- 100g unsalted butter, chilled and diced
- 1 tsp baking powder
- 1 tsp ground ginger
- 1/2 tsp ground cinnamon
- Pinch of salt
- 2 tbsp golden syrup
- 1-2 tbsp milk
- Demerara sugar, for sprinkling

1. Preheat your air fryer to 180°C (350°F).
2. In a large mixing bowl, combine the flour, caster sugar, baking powder, ginger, cinnamon, and salt.
3. Rub in the chilled, diced butter until the mixture resembles breadcrumbs.
4. Add the golden syrup and 1 tablespoon of milk, and stir until the mixture forms a stiff dough. If the mixture is too dry, add another tablespoon of milk.
5. Roll the dough into small balls, about the size of a walnut, and place them on a lined baking tray.
6. Using a fork, press down on the dough balls to flatten them slightly and create a criss-cross pattern.
7. Sprinkle the tops of the biscuits with Demerara sugar.
8. Place the tray in the air fryer and cook for 6-8 minutes, until the biscuits are golden brown.
9. Remove from the air fryer and allow to cool on the tray for 5 minutes before transferring to a wire rack to cool completely.
10. Enjoy your delicious air fryer Cornish fairings with a cup of tea!
11. Note: The cooking time may vary depending on the type and brand of air fryer used, so keep an eye on the biscuits and adjust the cooking time as needed.

Chapter 9
Tarts, Sandwiches, And Toasts

Bakewell Tart Recipe (Metric)

Bakewell tart is a classic English dessert that is loved for its delicious almond frangipane filling and shortcrust pastry base. Traditionally from the town of Bakewell in Derbyshire, this tart is a perfect tea-time treat or after-dinner dessert. In this recipe, we will show you how to make a Bakewell tart using an air fryer, resulting in a perfectly baked and crispy tart with a deliciously moist and flavorful filling.

Prep time: 15 minutes | Cook time: 45 minutes | Serves 4

- 200g plain flour
- 100g unsalted butter, chilled and diced
- 2-3 tbsp cold water
- 200g raspberry jam
- 100g ground almonds
- 100g caster sugar
- 2 large eggs
- 1 tsp almond extract
- Flaked almonds, to decorate
- Icing sugar, to dust

1. In a mixing bowl, combine the flour and butter using your fingertips until the mixture resembles fine breadcrumbs.
2. Add 2-3 tablespoons of cold water to the bowl and stir with a knife until the mixture comes together to form a dough. Knead the dough briefly and then wrap it in cling film and chill in the fridge for 30 minutes.
3. Preheat your air fryer to 160°C.
4. On a lightly floured surface, roll out the chilled pastry dough to a thickness of about 3mm.
5. Cut out the dough to fit your tart tin or mini tart tins, then line the tin with the pastry.
6. Prick the pastry base with a fork, then spread the raspberry jam over the pastry.
7. In a separate mixing bowl, combine the ground almonds, caster sugar, eggs, and almond extract.
8. Pour the almond mixture over the raspberry jam layer in the tart tin.
9. Sprinkle the flaked almonds over the top of the almond mixture.
10. Place the tart tin or tins into the preheated air fryer and cook for 15-20 minutes, or until the pastry is golden brown and the filling is set.
11. Once done, remove the tart from the air fryer and leave it to cool slightly before removing it from the tin.
12. Dust with icing sugar and serve warm or cold. Enjoy!

Cherry Bakewell Recipe (Metric)

Cherry Bakewell is a classic British dessert that is loved for its almond flavor and sweet cherry filling. This air fryer recipe puts a modern spin on the traditional recipe by using the air fryer to make a delicious and crispy crust. The cherry filling is made with fresh cherries and the almond flavor is enhanced with almond extract. This recipe is perfect for anyone looking for a quick and easy dessert that is sure to impress.

Prep time: 15 minutes | Cook time: 35 minutes | Serves 4

- 150g self-raising flour
- 50g ground almonds
- 125g unsalted butter, softened
- 125g caster sugar
- 2 large eggs
- 1 tsp almond extract
- 100g cherry jam
- 50g flaked almonds
- Icing sugar, to dust

1. In a bowl, whisk the softened butter and caster sugar until light and fluffy.
2. Gradually beat in the eggs, followed by the almond extract.
3. Add the flour and ground almonds and fold until just combined.
4. Spoon the mixture into an 18cm cake tin that will fit inside your air fryer basket.
5. Spread the cherry jam on top of the mixture and sprinkle with the flaked almonds.
6. Place the cake tin in the air fryer basket and cook at 160°C for 25-30 minutes or until a skewer inserted into the centre of the cake comes out clean.
7. Once the cake is cooked, carefully remove the tin from the air fryer and leave to cool for a few minutes.
8. Dust with icing sugar before serving.
9. Enjoy your delicious and easy Air Fryer Cherry Bakewell!

Gloucester Tart Recipe (Metric)

Gloucester Tart is a delicious traditional British dessert that originated in the city of Gloucester. The tart features a sweet pastry crust filled with a creamy, tangy mixture of cheese, sugar, and egg. This dessert is perfect for those who love a unique and satisfying flavor. In this recipe, we will be using an air fryer to make the tart, giving it a perfectly crisp crust and a smooth, creamy filling.

Prep time: 15 minutes | Cook time: 25 minutes| Serves 4

- 300g shortcrust pastry
- 125g butter
- 125g caster sugar
- 125g ground almonds
- 2 eggs, beaten
- 1 tablespoon of lemon juice
- 1 teaspoon of grated lemon zest
- 2 tablespoons of raspberry jam
- 50g flaked almonds

1. Preheat the air fryer to 180°C (356°F).
2. Roll out the pastry on a floured surface and use it to line a 20cm (8 inch) tart tin, trimming off any excess. Chill in the fridge for 15 minutes.
3. In a mixing bowl, cream together the butter and sugar until light and fluffy.
4. Add the ground almonds, beaten eggs, lemon juice and zest, and mix well.
5. Spread the raspberry jam evenly over the bottom of the pastry case.
6. Spoon the almond mixture over the jam, spreading it out evenly.
7. Sprinkle the flaked almonds over the top of the tart.
8. Place the tart tin in the air fryer basket and cook for 15-20 minutes, or until the filling is golden and firm to the touch.
9. Remove from the air fryer and allow to cool before slicing and serving.
10. Enjoy this delicious and traditional Gloucester tart in a quick and easy way with the air fryer!

Cheese-On-Toast (Metric)

Cheese-on-toast, also known as "Welsh rarebit," is a classic comfort food that is easy to make and satisfying to eat. It is a perfect quick meal for any time of day and can be customized with different types of cheese and toppings to suit your taste. This air fryer version of the recipe is quick and easy, resulting in perfectly melted cheese on crispy toast.

Prep time: 5 minutes | Cook time: 10 minutes| Serves 2

- 2 slices of bread
- 2-3 slices of cheddar cheese
- 1/4 teaspoon garlic powder
- Salt and black pepper to taste

1. Preheat the air fryer to 200°C.
2. Place the bread slices in the air fryer basket.
3. Air fry the bread slices for 2-3 minutes until they start to lightly toast.
4. Remove the basket from the air fryer and place the cheese slices on top of the bread slices.
5. Sprinkle the garlic powder, salt and pepper over the cheese slices.
6. Put the basket back in the air fryer and air fry for an additional 2-3 minutes, until the cheese is melted and bubbly.
7. Remove from the air fryer and serve hot.
8. Enjoy your delicious and easy Cheese-on-Toast made in the air fryer!

Easy Breakfast Toast (Metric)

It's quick, satisfying, and perfect for a busy morning when you need a filling meal to start your day. This air fryer recipe for spaghetti hoops on toast is a healthier twist on the classic dish, and it's sure to become a new favorite for the whole family.

Prep time: 5 minutes | Cook time: 15 minutes| Serves 3

- 4 slices of bread, preferably white
- 2 large eggs
- 50 ml whole milk
- 1 tsp sugar
- 1/2 tsp ground cinnamon
- 1/4 tsp salt
- 25 g unsalted butter, melted
- Maple syrup, honey, or jam for serving

1. Preheat the air fryer to 180°C.
2. In a bowl, whisk together the eggs, milk, sugar, cinnamon, and salt.
3. Dip each slice of bread in the egg mixture, coating it well on both sides.
4. Place the bread in the air fryer basket, making sure to leave some space between each slice.
5. Brush the melted butter over the top of each slice of bread.
6. Air fry the toast for 5-6 minutes, flipping halfway through, until golden brown and crispy.
7. Serve the toast immediately with your favorite topping, such as maple syrup, honey, or jam.
8. Enjoy your delicious English Toast made in the air fryer!

Baked Beans On Toast (Metric)

Baked beans on toast is a classic British dish that is popular for its simplicity, deliciousness, and affordability. It's a perfect breakfast, brunch, or even dinner option for those who are short on time but still want something satisfying and filling. In this air fryer recipe, we'll show you how to make baked beans on toast quickly and easily using the metric measurement, with the added benefit of a crispy toast that you won't get from stovetop cooking.

Prep time: 5 minutes | Cook time: 10 minutes| Serves 2

- 1 can of baked beans (400g)
- 1/4 onion, finely chopped
- 1/4 teaspoon paprika
- 1/4 teaspoon garlic powder
- Salt and pepper, to taste
- 2 slices of bread
- 1 tablespoon butter

1. Preheat the air fryer to 180°C.
2. In a small bowl, mix the baked beans, chopped onion, paprika, garlic powder, salt, and pepper.
3. Spread butter on both sides of the bread slices.
4. Place the bread slices in the air fryer basket and cook for 2-3 minutes or until lightly toasted.
5. Remove the bread slices from the air fryer and place on a plate.
6. Pour the baked beans mixture into the air fryer basket and cook for 3-4 minutes or until heated through.
7. Spoon the baked beans over the toast and serve.
8. Enjoy your quick and easy air fryer baked beans on toast!

Spaghetti Hoops On Toast (Metric)

Spaghetti hoops on toast is a classic British breakfast that is loved by children and adults alike. This simple and easy-to-make dish consists of spaghetti hoops (canned spaghetti in tomato sauce) on top of a slice of toasted bread.

Prep time: 5 minutes | Cook time: 8 minutes| Serves 3

- 4 slices of bread
- 1 can of spaghetti hoops
- 1 tbsp butter
- Salt and pepper, to taste

1. Preheat your air fryer to 180°C (350°F).
2. Toast your bread in the air fryer for 2-3 minutes until crispy.
3. In a small saucepan, heat the spaghetti hoops over medium heat for 2-3 minutes until warmed through.
4. Spread the butter on the toast and season with salt and pepper.
5. Spoon the spaghetti hoops onto the toast and serve immediately.

6. Enjoy your quick and easy Spaghetti Hoops on Toast made in the air fryer!

Bacon Sandwich (Metric)

Bacon sandwich, also known as a bacon butty or bacon sarnie, is a classic British breakfast dish loved by many. It is simple yet satisfying, featuring crispy bacon sandwiched between slices of soft bread. This air fryer recipe is a healthier twist on the traditional method of frying bacon, providing a delicious and easy way to enjoy this beloved breakfast sandwich.

Prep time: 5 minutes | Cook time: 10 minutes| Serves 3

- 4 slices of bread
- 8 strips of bacon
- 2 tablespoons of mayonnaise
- 2 teaspoons of Dijon mustard
- 2 lettuce leaves
- 2 slices of tomato
- Salt and pepper to taste

1. Preheat your air fryer to 390°F (200°C).
2. While the air fryer heats up, cook the bacon in a frying pan over medium-high heat until crispy. Set the bacon aside on a plate lined with paper towels to absorb excess grease.
3. In a small bowl, mix the mayonnaise and Dijon mustard together.
4. Place the bread slices in the air fryer basket and cook for 3-4 minutes until lightly toasted.
5. Remove the bread slices from the air fryer and spread the mayonnaise and Dijon mustard mixture onto one side of each slice.
6. Place a lettuce leaf and a slice of tomato onto two of the bread slices.
7. Divide the bacon strips between the two slices with the lettuce and tomato.
8. Season with salt and pepper to taste.
9. Top with the remaining bread slices to make the sandwiches.
10. Place the sandwiches back in the air fryer and cook for 1-2 minutes until the bread is crispy and the filling is heated through.
11. Serve hot and enjoy!

Note: You can also add other ingredients such as cheese or avocado to the sandwich if you prefer.

Chapter 10
Scottish Recipes

Neeps And Tatties (Turnips And Potatoes) (Metric)

Neeps and tatties is a traditional Scottish dish made with mashed turnips (neeps) and mashed potatoes (tatties). It's a hearty and comforting side dish that pairs perfectly with roasted meats, stews, or other Scottish dishes. This recipe has been adapted for the air fryer, which provides a quick and easy way to cook neeps and tatties without sacrificing any of the delicious flavor or texture.

Prep time: 15 minutes | Cook time: 25 minutes| Serves 4

- 400g turnips (neeps), peeled and chopped into small pieces
- 400g potatoes (tatties), peeled and chopped into small pieces
- 1 tablespoon olive oil
- Salt and pepper to taste

1. Preheat the air fryer to 200°C.
2. In a mixing bowl, toss the chopped turnips and potatoes with the olive oil until they are evenly coated.
3. Season with salt and pepper to taste.
4. Place the vegetables in the air fryer basket in a single layer, making sure they are not overcrowded.
5. Air fry for 15-20 minutes, shaking the basket occasionally to ensure even cooking.
6. Check the vegetables for doneness by piercing them with a fork. If they are tender, they are ready.
7. Serve hot as a side dish to your favorite meal.
8. Note: Cooking times may vary depending on the size of the vegetable pieces and the air fryer model. Adjust cooking time accordingly.

Recipe For Shortbread (Metric)

Shortbread is a classic Scottish dessert that is enjoyed all over the world. Its simple yet rich flavor and buttery texture make it a favorite treat for many. This air fryer recipe for shortbread is easy to follow and yields delicious results. Perfect for a snack, dessert or gifting to your loved ones!

Prep time: 15 minutes | Cook time: 40 minutes| Serves 4

- 200g unsalted butter, at room temperature
- 100g caster sugar
- 300g plain flour
- Pinch of salt

1. In a mixing bowl, cream the butter and caster sugar together until light and fluffy.
2. Sift the plain flour and salt into the bowl and mix until just combined.
3. Knead the dough gently until it forms a smooth ball.
4. Flatten the dough into a disc shape and wrap it in cling film.
5. Chill the dough in the fridge for at least 30 minutes.
6. Preheat your air fryer at 160°C for 5 minutes.
7. Roll the dough out on a floured surface to a thickness of about 1 cm.
8. Use a cookie cutter to cut out shapes and place them on a lined air fryer basket.
9. Air fry the shortbread for 10-12 minutes at 160°C or until golden brown.
10. Remove from the air fryer and allow to cool on a wire rack.
11. Enjoy your delicious homemade shortbread!

Scottish Salmon (Metric)

This air fryer Scottish Salmon recipe is a delicious and healthy option for dinner. With the help of an air fryer, this dish can be cooked quickly and with minimal mess. The flavorful marinade of soy sauce, honey, and lemon juice complements the natural taste of the salmon perfectly. This recipe is easy to follow and is sure to impress your family and guests.

Prep time: 15 minutes | Cook time: 20 minutes| Serves 4

- 4 Scottish salmon fillets (about 120g each)
- 2 tablespoons olive oil
- 2 tablespoons honey
- 1 tablespoon Dijon mustard
- 2 cloves garlic, minced
- 1 teaspoon dried thyme
- Salt and pepper, to taste

1. Preheat your air fryer to 180°C.
2. In a small bowl, whisk together the olive oil, honey, Dijon mustard, minced garlic, dried thyme, salt, and pepper.
3. Brush the salmon fillets with the honey mustard mixture, making sure they are evenly coated.
4. Place the salmon fillets in the air fryer basket, skin side down.
5. Cook for 8-10 minutes, depending on the thickness of the fillets. The salmon should be cooked through and flaky.
6. Serve the salmon fillets hot, garnished with fresh herbs or lemon wedges if desired.
7. Enjoy your delicious and healthy air fryer Scottish salmon!

A Full Scottish Breakfast (With Black Pudding) (Metric)

A Full Scottish breakfast is a hearty meal that typically includes various items such as eggs, bacon, sausages, black pudding, mushrooms, and tomatoes. It's a perfect way to start your day with a filling and nutritious meal. This air fryer recipe for a Full Scottish breakfast with black pudding is a healthier version that uses less oil without compromising on the taste and texture of the dish. It's quick, easy, and a great way to satisfy your cravings while keeping a watchful eye on your health.

Prep time: 15 minutes | Cook time: 25 minutes| Serves 4

- 4 pork sausages (approximately 400g)
- 4 rashers of bacon (approximately 200g)
- 4 black pudding slices (approximately 200g)
- 4 large eggs
- 2 medium-sized tomatoes, halved
- 4 mushrooms, halved
- 2 tattie scones (potato scones)
- 2-3 tablespoons of oil
- Salt and pepper to taste

1. Preheat the air fryer at 180°C for 3-5 minutes.
2. In a bowl, coat the tomatoes and mushrooms with a tablespoon of oil, salt, and pepper. Set them aside.
3. Place the sausages, bacon, black pudding, and tattie scones in the air fryer basket. Make sure they are not overlapping.
4. Cook for 6-7 minutes, then turn the ingredients over and cook for another 6-7 minutes. Make sure to check the meat's internal temperature with a thermometer, making sure it reaches 165°F or 74°C.
5. Remove the meat and tattie scones from the air fryer basket and transfer them to a serving plate.
6. Add the tomatoes and mushrooms to the air fryer basket, and cook for 3-4 minutes until tender and slightly charred.
7. Fry the eggs in a pan or use the air fryer to make sunny-side-up eggs.
8. Serve the Full Scottish breakfast hot with a cup of tea or coffee.
9. Enjoy your Full Scottish breakfast with black pudding cooked to perfection in your air fryer!

Scottish Oatcakes (Metric)

Scottish oatcakes are a traditional Scottish biscuit that are easy to make and perfect for snacking or serving as an appetizer with cheese or smoked salmon. This air fryer recipe for Scottish oatcakes uses metric measurements and is quick and simple to prepare, giving you a delicious and healthy snack in no time.

Prep time: 10 minutes | Cook time: 15 minutes| Serves 4

- 250g medium oatmeal
- 50g plain flour
- 1 tsp baking soda
- 1 tsp salt
- 50g unsalted butter, melted
- 150-200ml boiling water

1. In a large bowl, mix together the oatmeal, flour, baking soda and salt.
2. Add the melted butter to the bowl and mix until well combined.
3. Slowly pour in the boiling water, stirring the mixture until a dough forms. You may not need all of the water.
4. Preheat your air fryer to 180°C (350°F).
5. Roll out the dough on a lightly floured surface to a thickness of about 1cm.
6. Arrange the oatcakes in a single layer in the air fryer basket, leaving a little space between each one.
7. Remove the oatcakes from the air fryer and transfer them to a wire rack to cool completely.
8. These Scottish oatcakes can be enjoyed with cheese, butter, or any topping of your choice. They are a delicious and easy snack that can be made quickly in your air fryer.

Deep-Fried Mars Bar (Metric)

Deep-fried Mars Bars have gained popularity in recent years as a delicious and indulgent Scottish dessert. This decadent treat involves coating a Mars Bar in batter and deep-frying until it is crispy on the outside and gooey on the inside. With this air fryer recipe, you can now enjoy the same delicious taste of Deep-Fried Mars Bars with a slightly healthier twist. I would like to mention that a Deep-Fried Mars Bar is a dessert that is high in calories and not considered healthy. Please consume it in moderation.

Prep time: 15 minutes | Cook time: 15 minutes| Serves 4

- 1 Mars Bar
- 50g plain flour
- 1 tsp baking powder
- 1/4 tsp salt
- 1/4 tsp vanilla extract
- Vegetable oil spray

1. Preheat your air fryer to 200°C.
2. In a mixing bowl, whisk together the flour, baking powder, and salt.
3. Gradually add in the cold water and vanilla extract, stirring until the batter is smooth.
4. Cut the Mars Bar into bite-sized pieces.
5. Dip each piece into the batter, ensuring they are well-coated.
6. Place the coated Mars Bar pieces in the air fryer basket, making sure they are not touching each other.
7. Lightly spray the Mars Bar pieces with vegetable oil.
8. Air fry for 5-7 minutes, or until the batter is golden brown and crispy.
9. Remove from the air fryer and serve immediately.
10. Enjoy your Deep-Fried Mars Bars with caution and in moderation.

Chapter 11
British Cakes

Boxty Pancakes (Metric)

Boxty pancakes are a traditional Irish dish made from grated raw potatoes, mashed cooked potatoes, flour, and buttermilk. These hearty and filling pancakes are perfect for breakfast, brunch, or as a side dish. In this recipe, we'll be making Boxty pancakes in the air fryer, which yields a crispy exterior and a fluffy interior, without the need for flipping or greasy frying. The recipe is easy to make and perfect for those who love a savory breakfast.

Prep time: 5 minutes | Cook time: 15 minutes| Serves 2

- 200g grated raw potatoes
- 200g mashed potatoes
- 100g all-purpose flour
- 1 tsp baking powder
- 1 tsp salt
- 1 egg
- 150ml milk
- 1 tbsp butter

1. In a large bowl, combine grated raw potatoes, mashed potatoes, flour, baking powder, and salt.
2. Add the egg and milk to the mixture and stir until well combined.
3. Preheat the air fryer to 200°C (400°F).
4. Grease the air fryer basket with butter.
5. Drop 2-3 tablespoons of the mixture onto the basket to form a pancake.
6. Cook the pancakes for 5-6 minutes until they are golden brown and crispy on the outside.
7. Flip the pancakes halfway through cooking to ensure they cook evenly.
8. Repeat the process until all the batter is used up.
9. Serve the Boxty pancakes hot with your preferred toppings such as butter, sour cream, or smoked salmon.
10. Enjoy your delicious and healthy Boxty pancakes made with the air fryer!

Yorkshire Parkin (Metric)

Yorkshire parkin is a traditional gingerbread-like cake from Northern England. It is often served during Bonfire Night, a popular autumn celebration in the UK. Parkin is a sticky and dense cake made with oats, treacle, and spices like ginger and nutmeg. The cake is often eaten with a dollop of whipped cream or a slice of cheese. This air fryer recipe is a quick and easy way to make this delicious treat, with the added bonus of a crispy crust from the air fryer.

Prep time: 15 minutes | Cook time: 1 hour 10 minutes| Serves 6

- 250g medium oatmeal
- 125g self-raising flour
- 1 tsp baking powder
- 1 tsp ground ginger
- 1 tsp mixed spice
- 200g butter
- 200g black treacle
- 200g golden syrup
- 200g dark brown sugar
- 2 eggs, beaten
- 100ml milk

1. Preheat your air fryer to 160°C (320°F).
2. In a large mixing bowl, combine the oatmeal, self-raising flour, baking powder, ground ginger, and mixed spice.
3. In a saucepan, melt the butter, black treacle, golden syrup, and dark brown sugar over low heat. Stir until smooth.
4. Pour the melted mixture into the dry ingredients and mix well.
5. Add the beaten eggs and milk to the mixture, and stir until everything is combined.
6. Grease a square cake tin and pour in the mixture.
7. Place the cake tin in the air fryer and cook for 40-45 minutes, or until a skewer inserted into the center of the cake comes out clean.
8. Remove the cake from the air fryer and allow it to cool in the tin for 10 minutes.
9. Once cooled, remove the cake from the tin and cut it into squares.
10. Serve and enjoy your delicious Yorkshire Parkin!

Welsh Cakes (Metric)

Welsh cakes, also known as griddle cakes, are a traditional Welsh teatime treat that are quick and easy to make. These sweet, spiced cakes are made with flour, butter, sugar, and currants, and are cooked on a griddle or in a frying pan. In this recipe, we'll show you how to make Welsh cakes using an air fryer, which results in a lighter and healthier version of this classic snack. They're perfect for serving with a cup of tea or coffee, and are sure to be a hit with the whole family.

Prep time: 15 minutes | Cook time: 10 minutes| Serves 4

- 225g self-raising flour
- 110g unsalted butter, cold and cut into small cubes
- 85g caster sugar
- 1/4 tsp mixed spice
- 1/4 tsp ground cinnamon
- 1/4 tsp baking powder
- 50g currants
- 1 egg, beaten
- Milk, if needed
- Icing sugar, for dusting

1. In a mixing bowl, add the flour, sugar, mixed spice, cinnamon, and baking powder. Mix well.
2. Add the cubed butter and rub it into the dry ingredients using your fingertips until the mixture resembles breadcrumbs.
3. Add the currants and mix well.
4. Add the beaten egg to the mixture and mix until it forms a soft dough. If the mixture seems dry, add a splash of milk to bring it together.
5. Roll the dough out on a lightly floured surface to a thickness of around 5mm.
6. Using a 6-7cm round cutter, cut out as many rounds as you can from the dough.
7. Preheat the air fryer to 180°C.
8. Place the rounds of dough in the air fryer basket, making sure not to overcrowd them.
9. Cook for 2-3 minutes on each side until golden brown and cooked through.
10. Remove the Welsh Cakes from the air fryer and transfer to a wire rack to cool.
11. Dust with icing sugar before serving.
12. Enjoy your delicious Welsh Cakes made in the air fryer!

Eccles Cake (Metric)

Eccles cakes are a traditional British pastry that originated in the town of Eccles in Greater Manchester. These sweet treats are made with flaky pastry filled with a mixture of currants, sugar, and spices. They are perfect for serving with a cup of tea or coffee as an afternoon snack. In this air fryer recipe, we'll show you how to make these delicious Eccles cakes using metric measurements and without having to turn on your oven.

Prep time: 15 minutes | Cook time: 15 minutes| Serves 4

- 250g puff pastry
- 100g unsalted butter, softened
- 100g caster sugar
- 150g currants
- 1 tsp ground cinnamon
- 1/2 tsp ground nutmeg
- 1 egg, beaten

1. Preheat the air fryer to 180°C.
2. In a bowl, mix together the softened butter, caster sugar, currants, ground cinnamon, and ground nutmeg.
3. On a floured surface, roll out the puff pastry to a thickness of about 3mm.
4. Using a 10cm round cutter, cut out circles from the pastry.
5. Place a spoonful of the currant mixture in the center of each pastry circle.
6. Brush the edges of the pastry with beaten egg and fold over to enclose the currant mixture, pinching the edges to seal.
7. Turn the Eccles cakes over and flatten them slightly with the palm of your hand.
8. Place the Eccles cakes in the air fryer basket, making sure to leave some space between them.
9. Air fry for 8-10 minutes or until golden brown and crispy.
10. Remove the Eccles cakes from the air fryer and allow them to cool for a few minutes before serving.
11. Enjoy your homemade Eccles cakes!

Fresh Cherry Cake (Metric)

Fresh cherry cake is a delicious dessert that is perfect for any occasion. This moist and fluffy cake is made with fresh cherries that give it a delightful burst of fruity flavor. Baked to perfection in an air fryer, this cake is quick and easy to make, and can be enjoyed on its own or with a dollop of whipped cream. This recipe is perfect for anyone who loves baking and wants to try something new in their air fryer.

Prep time: 15 minutes | Cook time: 55 minutes | Serves 4

- 200g all-purpose flour
- 1 tsp baking powder
- 1/2 tsp baking soda
- 1/4 tsp salt
- 100g unsalted butter, at room temperature
- 150g granulated sugar
- 2 large eggs
- 1/2 tsp vanilla extract
- 120ml milk
- 200g fresh cherries, pitted and chopped

1. In a medium bowl, whisk together the flour, baking powder, baking soda, and salt.
2. In a large bowl, beat the butter and sugar together until light and fluffy. Add the eggs one at a time, beating well after each addition. Stir in the vanilla extract.
3. Gradually add the flour mixture to the butter mixture, alternating with the milk and mixing well after each addition.
4. Fold in the chopped cherries.
5. Preheat the air fryer to 160°C (320°F).
6. Grease a 7-inch cake pan with cooking spray and pour the batter into the pan.
7. Place the pan in the air fryer basket and cook for 30-35 minutes, or until a toothpick inserted in the center of the cake comes out clean.
8. Let the cake cool for 10 minutes before removing it from the pan and transferring it to a wire rack to cool completely.
9. Slice and serve.
10. Enjoy your delicious air fryer fresh cherry cake!

Victoria Sponge Cake Recipe (Metric)

Victoria Sponge Cake is a classic British cake that is simple yet elegant. It consists of two layers of soft and fluffy sponge cake sandwiched together with sweet jam and whipped cream. This cake is perfect for any occasion, from a casual afternoon tea to a special celebration. In this air fryer recipe, we'll show you how to make a delicious Victoria Sponge Cake using metric measurements, so you can easily recreate this British classic at home.

Prep time: 5 minutes | Cook time: 15 minutes | Serves 4

- 225g unsalted butter, softened
- 225g caster sugar
- 4 large eggs
- 225g self-raising flour
- 2 tbsp milk
- 1 tsp vanilla extract
- 150g raspberry jam
- Icing sugar, for dusting

1. Preheat the air fryer to 160°C (320°F).
2. In a large mixing bowl, cream the softened butter and caster sugar together until light and fluffy.
3. Add the eggs, one at a time, mixing well after each addition.
4. Sift in the self-raising flour and gently fold it into the mixture.
5. Add the milk and vanilla extract, and mix until the batter is smooth and creamy.
6. Grease two 18cm (7 inch) cake tins with butter and divide the cake batter equally between them.
7. Place the cake tins in the air fryer basket and cook for 15-20 minutes or until the cakes are golden brown and a toothpick inserted into the center comes out clean.
8. Once cooked, remove the cake tins from the air fryer basket and let them cool for 5 minutes.
9. Remove the cakes from the tins and let them cool completely on a wire rack.
10. Once the cakes have cooled, spread the raspberry jam on one of the cakes and place the other cake on top.
11. Dust the top of the cake with icing sugar before serving.
12. Enjoy your delicious air fryer Victoria Sponge Cake!

Banbury Cake Recipe (Metric)

This air fryer Banbury Cake recipe is a delicious twist on the classic English cake. Made with a flaky pastry dough and filled with a sweet mixture of currants, raisins, and candied peel, this cake is perfect for a snack or a special occasion. Using an air fryer instead of an oven makes it quicker and easier to prepare, with the added bonus of a crispy crust and a moist, flavorful filling.

Prep time: 15 minutes | Cook time: 25 minutes| Serves 4

- 250g plain flour
- 1 tsp baking powder
- 1 tsp ground cinnamon
- 1/2 tsp ground nutmeg
- 125g unsalted butter, softened
- 125g light brown sugar
- 1 medium egg
- 75g raisins
- 75g currants
- 75g candied peel
- 2 tbsp milk
- Icing sugar, for dusting

1. In a mixing bowl, sift the flour, baking powder, cinnamon and nutmeg together. Set aside.
2. In another mixing bowl, cream the butter and sugar together until light and fluffy.
3. Add the egg to the butter mixture and beat well.
4. Gradually add the flour mixture to the butter mixture, mixing until a stiff dough is formed.
5. Stir in the raisins, currants, candied peel, and milk until everything is evenly combined.
6. Preheat your air fryer to 160°C (320°F).
7. Divide the dough into 6 to 8 portions and shape each portion into a round cake, about 1 inch thick and 3 inches in diameter.
8. Place the cakes into the air fryer basket, leaving a little space between each one.
9. Cook the cakes in the air fryer for 12-15 minutes until they are golden brown and firm to the touch.
10. Remove the cakes from the air fryer and let them cool on a wire rack.
11. Once cooled, dust with icing sugar before serving.
12. Enjoy your delicious Banbury Cakes!

Note: Cooking times and temperatures may vary depending on the model and brand of air fryer.

Battenberg Cake Recipe (Metric)

Battenberg Cake is a classic British dessert that features a distinctive checkerboard pattern and is typically made with almond sponge cake and marzipan. This delicious cake is perfect for any occasion, from afternoon tea to birthday parties. In this recipe, we will be using an air fryer to create a moist and fluffy cake with a perfect texture and a beautiful marzipan layer. It's a fun and easy way to make a show-stopping dessert that will impress your guests!

Prep time: 15 minutes | Cook time: 35 minutes| Serves 4

- 175g unsalted butter, softened
- 175g caster sugar
- 3 large eggs
- 175g self-raising flour
- 1 tsp vanilla extract
- 1 tsp almond extract
- 1 tbsp milk
- Red food colouring
- 1/4 cup apricot jam
- 400g marzipan

1. Preheat the air fryer to 160°C.
2. In a large mixing bowl, cream the softened butter and caster sugar together until pale and fluffy.
3. Gradually add the eggs, beating well after each addition.
4. Fold in the self-raising flour, vanilla extract, almond extract and milk until the mixture is smooth and fully combined.
5. Divide the mixture equally into two bowls.
6. Add a few drops of red food colouring to one bowl and mix well to make a pink mixture.
7. Grease a square baking tin (20cm x 20cm) with oil or cooking spray.
8. Place a piece of parchment paper on the bottom of the baking tin.
9. Spoon the pink mixture into one half of the tin, and the white mixture into the other half.
10. Bake in the air fryer for 20-25 minutes until the sponge is cooked through and golden on top.
11. Leave the sponge to cool completely.
12. Meanwhile, roll out the marzipan on a flat surface dusted with icing sugar.
13. Warm up the apricot jam in a saucepan over low heat until it becomes runny.
14. Spread the jam on top of the pink sponge and place the white sponge on top of the jam.
15. Brush the rest of the jam over the top and sides of the cake.
16. Place the rolled-out marzipan on top of the cake and fold the excess over the sides.
17. Cut the cake into slices and serve.
18. Enjoy your delicious homemade Air Fryer Battenberg Cake!

Dundee Cake Recipe (Metric)

Dundee Cake is a classic Scottish fruitcake that is packed with flavor and perfect for any occasion. This cake is made with a rich combination of dried fruit, almonds, and spices, making it a popular choice during the festive season. In this air fryer recipe, we'll show you how to make a delicious and moist Dundee Cake in no time. So, let's get started!

Prep time: 15 minutes | Cook time: 55 minutes| Serves 6

- 200g unsalted butter, at room temperature
- 200g caster sugar
- 4 large eggs
- 200g self-raising flour
- 100g ground almonds
- 50g mixed peel
- 150g raisins
- 150g sultanas
- Zest of 1 lemon
- Zest of 1 orange
- 2 tablespoons of milk
- Whole blanched almonds, for decoration

1. Preheat the air fryer to 160°C.
2. Grease a 6-inch cake tin and line the bottom and sides with parchment paper.
3. In a large mixing bowl, cream together the butter and sugar until light and fluffy.
4. Gradually beat in the eggs, one at a time.
5. Add the flour and ground almonds, and mix until just combined.
6. Fold in the mixed peel, raisins, sultanas, lemon zest, orange zest, and milk.
7. Pour the mixture into the prepared cake tin and smooth the top with a spatula.
8. Decorate the top of the cake with whole blanched almonds in a circular pattern.
9. Place the cake tin into the air fryer basket and cook for 40-50 minutes, or until a skewer inserted into the center of the cake comes out clean.
10. Once cooked, remove the cake from the air fryer and allow it to cool in the tin for 10 minutes.
11. Turn the cake out onto a wire rack to cool completely before serving.
12. Enjoy your delicious air fryer Dundee Cake!

Banbury Cakes Recipe (Metric)

Banbury cakes are a type of pastry filled with dried fruits and spices that originated in the town of Banbury, England. They are a delicious treat that can be enjoyed any time of day, and this air fryer recipe is a quick and easy way to make them using the metric measurement. With a crispy exterior and a warm, fruity filling, these Banbury cakes are sure to be a hit with everyone.

Prep time: 15 minutes | Cook time: 25 minutes| Serves 4

- 200g all-purpose flour
- 100g unsalted butter, chilled and diced
- 60g currants
- 50g light brown sugar
- 25g mixed candied peel
- 1/2 tsp ground cinnamon
- 1/4 tsp ground nutmeg
- 1/4 tsp ground allspice
- 1/4 tsp salt
- 3-4 tbsp water
- 1 egg, beaten
- Granulated sugar, for sprinkling

1. In a mixing bowl, combine the flour, cinnamon, nutmeg, allspice, salt, and light brown sugar.
2. Add the chilled, diced butter to the dry ingredients and use your fingertips to rub the mixture together until it resembles fine breadcrumbs.
3. Stir in the currants and mixed candied peel.
4. Gradually add the water, one tablespoon at a time, stirring the mixture with a knife until it forms a stiff dough.
5. Roll out the dough on a floured surface to about 3mm thickness and cut out 10cm rounds using a pastry cutter.
6. Brush the edges of the rounds with beaten egg.
7. Mix together some of the leftover egg with a little water to make an egg wash.
8. Spoon a small amount of the filling in the center of each round.
9. Fold the pastry over to create a half-moon shape and crimp the edges to seal.
10. Brush the top of each cake with the egg wash and sprinkle with granulated sugar.
11. Preheat the air fryer to 180°C.
12. Place the cakes in the air fryer basket and cook for 10-12 minutes until golden brown.
13. Allow the Banbury cakes to cool before serving.
14. Enjoy your freshly baked air fryer Banbury cakes!

Coffee And Walnut Cake (Metric)

This air fryer Coffee and Walnut Cake is a delicious and easy-to-make dessert that will satisfy your sweet tooth. Made with rich coffee flavor and crunchy walnuts, this cake is perfect for coffee lovers who enjoy a subtle nutty flavor. The air fryer method ensures a moist and fluffy texture, and the recipe is simple enough to follow even if you're new to baking. Treat yourself to a slice of this delicious cake, and enjoy it with a cup of tea or coffee for a perfect afternoon treat.

Prep time: 15 minutes | Cook time: 35 minutes | Serves 4

- 175g unsalted butter, softened
- 175g caster sugar
- 3 large eggs
- 175g self-raising flour
- 1 1/2 tbsp instant coffee granules, dissolved in 1 tbsp boiling water
- 50g walnuts, roughly chopped
- For the frosting:
- 100g unsalted butter, softened
- 200g icing sugar
- 1 1/2 tsp instant coffee granules, dissolved in 1 tbsp boiling water
- 25g walnuts, roughly chopped

1. Preheat your air fryer to 160°C (320°F).
2. Grease a 6-inch round cake tin and line the bottom with parchment paper.
3. In a large mixing bowl, beat the butter and sugar together until light and fluffy.
4. Gradually beat in the eggs, one at a time.
5. Sift the flour into the bowl and gently fold into the mixture until fully combined.
6. Stir in the dissolved coffee and chopped walnuts.
7. Spoon the mixture into the prepared cake tin and smooth the surface with a spatula.
8. Place the tin in the air fryer basket and cook for 25-30 minutes, or until a toothpick inserted into the center of the cake comes out clean.
9. Remove the cake from the air fryer and leave it to cool completely on a wire rack.
10. To make the frosting, beat the butter, icing sugar, and dissolved coffee together in a mixing bowl until smooth and creamy.
11. Spread the frosting evenly over the cooled cake with a spatula.
12. Sprinkle the chopped walnuts on top of the frosting.
13. Slice and serve.
14. Note: Cooking times may vary depending on the brand and model of your air fryer. Check the cake frequently towards the end of the cooking time to prevent overcooking or burning.

Carrot Cake Recipe (Metric)

Carrot cake is a classic and delicious dessert that everyone loves. It is a moist and flavorful cake made with grated carrots, nuts, and warm spices. This air fryer recipe for carrot cake is perfect for those who want to enjoy a homemade treat without having to turn on the oven. The air fryer ensures that the cake is evenly cooked and the crust is crispy. This recipe is easy to make and yields a delicious cake that can be enjoyed with a cup of tea or coffee.

Prep time: 15 minutes | Cook time: 45 minutes | Serves 4

- 200g self-raising flour
- 1 tsp baking powder
- 1 tsp ground cinnamon
- 1/2 tsp ground ginger
- 1/4 tsp ground nutmeg
- 1/2 tsp salt
- 175g light brown sugar
- 2 large eggs
- 125ml vegetable oil
- 1 tsp vanilla extract
- 200g grated carrots
- 50g chopped walnuts (optional)
- For Cream Cheese Frosting:
- 100g cream cheese
- 50g unsalted butter, softened
- 200g powdered sugar
- 1/2 tsp vanilla extract

1. In a medium bowl, whisk together the flour, baking powder, cinnamon, ginger, nutmeg, and salt.
2. In a separate large bowl, beat the sugar, eggs, oil, and vanilla extract until well combined.
3. Gradually fold in the flour mixture into the wet ingredients, making sure everything is well combined.
4. Stir in the grated carrots and chopped walnuts until evenly distributed.
5. Preheat your air fryer to 160°C.
6. Grease an 18cm round cake pan with cooking spray, then pour the cake batter into the pan.
7. Place the cake pan into the air fryer basket and cook for 25-30 minutes, or until a toothpick inserted into the center of the cake comes out clean.
8. Allow the cake to cool in the pan for 10 minutes, then transfer it to a wire rack to cool completely.
9. To make the cream cheese frosting, beat the cream cheese and butter until smooth and creamy. Gradually add in the powdered sugar and vanilla extract, and continue to beat until well combined.
10. Once the cake has cooled, spread the cream cheese frosting evenly over the top of the cake.
11. Cut into slices and serve. Enjoy your delicious air fryer carrot cake!

Madeira Cake Recipe (Metric)

Madeira cake is a classic British tea time treat that's easy to make and perfect for serving with a cup of tea or coffee. This buttery, dense cake has a slight lemony flavor and a lovely moist texture. It's a versatile cake that can be enjoyed on its own, topped with a drizzle of icing or jam, or served as the base for a trifle. In this recipe, we'll show you how to make Madeira cakes in the air fryer, which is a quick and convenient way to enjoy this delicious cake.

Prep time: 15 minutes | Cook time: 45 minutes| Serves 4

- 200g unsalted butter, softened
- 200g caster sugar
- 200g self-raising flour
- 1 tsp baking powder
- 4 large eggs
- 2 tbsp milk
- Zest of 1 lemon

1. Preheat your air fryer to 160°C.
2. Grease a 7-inch cake tin and line it with parchment paper.
3. In a mixing bowl, cream the softened butter and sugar until light and fluffy.
4. Add the eggs, one at a time, and mix well after each addition.
5. Sift in the self-raising flour and baking powder, and fold them into the mixture gently.
6. Add the milk and lemon zest to the mixture and mix until fully combined.
7. Pour the batter into the prepared cake tin and smooth the top.
8. Place the cake tin in the air fryer and cook for 35-40 minutes, or until a skewer inserted into the center of the cake comes out clean.
9. Remove the cake from the air fryer and let it cool in the tin for 5 minutes.
10. Transfer the cake onto a wire rack to cool completely.
11. Slice and serve the Madeira cake with your favorite topping, such as whipped cream and fresh berries.
12. Enjoy your delicious Madeira cake made in an air fryer!

Chorley Cake Recipe (Metric)

Chorley cake is a traditional pastry from the town of Chorley in Lancashire, England. These small, flat cakes are filled with currants or raisins and have a buttery, flaky texture. They're often enjoyed as a snack or served with tea. In this air fryer recipe, we'll show you how to make delicious Chorley cakes using metric measurements and your trusty air fryer.

Prep time: 15 minutes | Cook time: 20 minutes| Serves 4

- 250g plain flour
- 1 tsp baking powder
- 1/4 tsp salt
- 50g caster sugar
- 100g unsalted butter, diced
- 75g currants
- 25g candied peel
- 1/2 tsp ground allspice
- 1 egg, beaten
- 2 tbsp milk
- Demerara sugar, for sprinkling

1. Preheat your air fryer to 180°C (350°F).
2. In a large mixing bowl, combine the flour, baking powder, salt, and caster sugar.
3. Add the diced butter to the bowl and rub it into the dry ingredients using your fingertips until the mixture resembles breadcrumbs.
4. Add the currants, candied peel, and ground allspice to the bowl and stir to combine.
5. In a separate small bowl, beat the egg and milk together.
6. Add the egg mixture to the dry ingredients and mix until it forms a dough.
7. Roll out the dough on a floured surface to a thickness of around 1cm.
8. Cut the dough into circles using a cookie cutter or glass.
9. Place the circles onto a greased air fryer tray, leaving a little space between them.
10. Sprinkle each circle with a little Demerara sugar.
11. Air fry for 8-10 minutes, until the cakes are lightly golden and cooked through.
12. Remove from the air fryer and let cool on a wire rack before serving.
13. Enjoy your freshly baked Chorley cakes from the air fryer!

Chelsea Buns (Metric)

Chelsea buns are a classic British sweet bun made with a rich, spiced dough, filled with currants, sugar, and butter, and rolled up into a spiral shape. They are often served with a sticky glaze and are a popular treat for breakfast or afternoon tea. This air fryer recipe for Chelsea buns using metric measurements is a quick and easy way to make these delicious buns with a crispy outer layer and a soft, gooey center.

Prep time: 15 minutes | Cook time: 20 minutes| Serves 4

- 500g plain flour
- 7g instant yeast
- 50g caster sugar
- 1 tsp salt
- 1 egg
- 60g unsalted butter, melted
- 250ml warm milk
- 100g dried mixed fruit
- 1 tsp ground cinnamon
- 50g unsalted butter, softened
- 50g caster sugar
- 1 egg, beaten
- 2 tbsp apricot jam
- 2 tbsp boiling water

1. In a large bowl, mix together the flour, yeast, sugar, and salt. Add in the egg, melted butter, and warm milk, and stir until the dough comes together.
2. Turn the dough out onto a floured surface and knead for 10 minutes until it becomes smooth and elastic.
3. Place the dough in a greased bowl, cover with a damp cloth, and let it rise for 1 hour in a warm place.
4. Preheat the air fryer to 180°C.
5. Roll out the dough into a rectangle shape, roughly 30cm x 20cm.
6. Mix together the dried fruit and cinnamon, then sprinkle it evenly over the dough.
7. Spread the softened butter over the top of the fruit and sprinkle the caster sugar over it.
8. Roll the dough up from the longest edge, to create a spiral shape.
9. Cut the roll into 12 even slices and place them cut-side down in the air fryer basket, leaving space between each slice.
10. Brush the beaten egg over the buns and cook in the air fryer for 10-12 minutes, until golden brown.
11. Mix together the apricot jam and boiling water to make a glaze, and brush over the hot buns. Serve warm.
12. Enjoy your delicious and fluffy Chelsea Buns made in the air fryer!

Queen Elizabeth Cakes Recipe (Metric)

Queen Elizabeth Cakes are a delicious and elegant treat that is perfect for tea time or special occasions. Made with a buttery sponge cake, filled with sweet raspberry jam and topped with a layer of icing and a cherry, these small cakes are sure to impress. This air fryer recipe allows you to make these cakes easily and quickly, while still achieving the same delicious and delicate texture as the oven-baked version.

Prep time: 15 minutes | Cook time: 20 minutes| Serves 4

- 120g unsalted butter, softened
- 100g caster sugar
- 2 medium eggs
- 1 tsp vanilla extract
- 200g self-raising flour
- 1/2 tsp baking powder
- 80g chopped dates
- 50g chopped walnuts

1. In a large mixing bowl, cream together the softened butter and caster sugar until light and fluffy.
2. Beat in the eggs one at a time, then stir in the vanilla extract.
3. Sift in the self-raising flour and baking powder, and fold the mixture together until well combined.
4. Stir in the chopped dates and walnuts until evenly distributed.
5. Preheat the air fryer to 160°C.
6. Spoon the mixture into a muffin tin lined with paper cases, filling each one about 2/3 full.
7. Place the muffin tin into the preheated air fryer basket and cook for 12-15 minutes, or until the cakes are risen and golden brown on top.
8. Remove the muffin tin from the air fryer and allow the cakes to cool in the tin for a few minutes before transferring to a wire rack to cool completely.
9. Enjoy your delicious Queen Elizabeth Cakes made in the air fryer!

French Fancies (Metric)

French fancies are delightful little cakes that are a favourite of many people. These mini sponge cakes are topped with delicious buttercream and coated in a layer of fondant icing, making them the perfect sweet treat for any occasion. In this air fryer recipe, we will show you how to make these delicious French fancies easily and quickly. With the help of your air fryer, you can enjoy these little cakes in no time at all.

Prep time: 15 minutes | Cook time: 25 minutes| Serves 4

- 110g unsalted butter, softened
- 110g caster sugar
- 2 medium eggs
- 110g self-raising flour
- 1/2 tsp baking powder
- 1/2 tsp vanilla extract
- Food colouring (pink, yellow, and white)
- 300g fondant icing
- Sprinkles (optional)

1. In a mixing bowl, cream the butter and sugar together until light and fluffy.
2. Add the eggs one at a time, beating well after each addition.
3. Sift the flour and baking powder into the mixture, and fold gently until combined. Add in the vanilla extract and mix.
4. Line a 6-inch square baking pan with parchment paper, then transfer the cake batter into it. Smooth the top with a spatula.
5. Preheat the air fryer at 160°C (320°F) for 5 minutes.
6. Place the baking pan in the air fryer basket and bake for 15-20 minutes, or until the cake is fully cooked through.
7. Once done, remove the pan from the air fryer and let it cool for 10 minutes before transferring it to a wire rack to cool completely.
8. Using a sharp knife, cut the cake into small rectangular shapes.
9. Divide the fondant icing into three equal portions and color each portion with pink, yellow, and white food coloring.
10. Take one piece of cake and place it on a fork. Spoon the fondant icing over the cake, making sure it is coated on all sides. Tap off any excess icing and transfer to a wire rack to dry.
11. Repeat the process with the remaining cake pieces and fondant icing. If desired, sprinkle some sprinkles on top before the icing dries.
12. Let the icing set for at least an hour before serving.
13. Enjoy your delicious air fryer French Fancies!

Simnel Cakes Recipe (Metric)

These traditional Simnel Cakes are a delicious treat that can be enjoyed any time of the year, but are particularly popular during Easter. Made with a rich fruitcake base and topped with almond paste, these cakes are a true delight. This air fryer recipe is a quick and easy way to make these cakes without the need for an oven, and the use of metric measurements makes it easy to follow along. Give it a try and enjoy the taste of this classic treat in no time!

Prep time: 15 minutes | Cook time: 20 minutes| Serves 4

- 200g mixed dried fruit
- 100g unsalted butter, softened
- 100g light brown sugar
- 2 large eggs, beaten
- 150g self-raising flour
- 1/2 tsp mixed spice
- 1/2 tsp ground cinnamon
- 1/2 lemon, zest only
- 200g almond paste
- 1 egg yolk, beaten
- Icing sugar, for dusting

1. Preheat the air fryer to 160°C.
2. In a bowl, mix together the dried fruit, flour, mixed spice, cinnamon, and lemon zest until well combined.
3. In a separate bowl, cream together the butter and sugar until light and fluffy.
4. Gradually beat in the eggs, a little at a time, until well combined.
5. Fold in the dry ingredients until everything is well mixed together.
6. Divide the mixture into 11 equal-sized balls and flatten them slightly to form discs.
7. Place the discs in the air fryer basket and cook for 12-15 minutes or until lightly golden.
8. Remove the cakes from the air fryer and leave to cool completely.
9. Roll out the almond paste on a surface dusted with icing sugar until it's about 3mm thick.
10. Using a cookie cutter, cut out 11 circles and place them on top of the cooled cakes.
11. Brush the tops of the cakes with beaten egg yolk.
12. Preheat the air fryer to 180°C and cook the cakes for 2-3 minutes or until the almond paste is lightly golden.
13. Remove the cakes from the air fryer and leave to cool before serving.

Chapter 12
Christmas Recipe

Roast Potatoes (Metric)

Roast potatoes are a classic side dish that complement many meals, especially during holidays and special occasions. Crispy on the outside and fluffy on the inside, they are the perfect accompaniment to a roast dinner. This air fryer recipe for roast potatoes will guide you through the steps to achieve perfectly cooked and seasoned potatoes that everyone will enjoy.

Prep time: 15 minutes | Cook time: 25 minutes| Serves 4

- 800g potatoes, peeled and chopped into small chunks
- 2 tbsp vegetable oil
- 1 tsp garlic powder
- 1 tsp paprika
- 1 tsp dried thyme
- Salt and pepper, to taste

1. Preheat the air fryer to 200°C.
2. In a bowl, mix together the chopped potatoes, vegetable oil, garlic powder, paprika, thyme, salt, and pepper.
3. Once well combined, transfer the potato mixture to the air fryer basket.
4. Cook the potatoes for 20-25 minutes, shaking the basket occasionally to ensure even cooking.
5. Once the potatoes are golden and crispy, remove them from the air fryer and serve hot.
6. Enjoy your delicious and crispy air fryer roast potatoes!

Pigs In Blankets (Metric)

Pigs in blankets are a classic appetizer or side dish that are loved by many. This air fryer version makes it even easier and quicker to make this delicious treat. With only a few simple ingredients and the magic of the air fryer, you can have crispy and savory pigs in blankets in no time. They're perfect for parties, game day snacks, or even just a quick and easy weeknight dinner.

Prep time: 15 minutes | Cook time: 20 minutes| Serves 4

- 8 pork sausages
- 8 rashers of streaky bacon
- 1 tbsp olive oil
- Salt and pepper

1. Preheat the air fryer to 200°C.
2. Wrap each sausage in a rasher of bacon, making sure the ends of the bacon are tucked under the sausage.
3. Brush the pigs in blankets with olive oil and season with salt and pepper.
4. Place the pigs in blankets in the air fryer basket in a single layer.
5. Cook for 10-12 minutes, flipping halfway through, until the bacon is crispy and the sausages are cooked through.
6. Remove from the air fryer and serve hot.
7. Enjoy your delicious Pigs in Blankets made in the air fryer!

Yorkshire Pudding (Metric)

This recipe is for the classic British dish of Yorkshire pudding made in an air fryer using metric measurements. These crispy and fluffy golden-brown puddings are perfect as a side dish for a Sunday roast or any other hearty meal. They are easy to make and can be ready in no time with the help of an air fryer.

Prep time: 5 minutes | Cook time: 15 minutes| Serves 4

- 100g plain flour
- 2 medium eggs
- 150ml milk
- 1/2 tsp salt
- 1/2 tsp pepper
- 2 tbsp vegetable oil

1. Preheat your air fryer to 200°C.
2. In a mixing bowl, whisk together the flour, eggs, and milk until you have a smooth batter.
3. Add the salt and pepper to the batter and whisk again.
4. Divide the oil evenly among the silicone cupcake cases, then place the cases into the air fryer for 3 minutes to heat up the oil.
5. Once the oil is hot, remove the cupcake cases from the air fryer and pour the batter evenly into each case.
6. Return the cupcake cases to the air fryer and cook for 12 minutes, or until the puddings are puffed up and golden brown.
7. Remove the Yorkshire puddings from the air fryer and serve hot with your favorite roast beef and gravy.
8. Enjoy your delicious and fluffy Yorkshire Puddings made in the air fryer!

Christmas Pudding (Metric)

Christmas pudding is a traditional British dessert that is typically served during the holiday season. Also known as plum pudding, it is a rich and decadent dessert made with dried fruits, spices, and brandy or rum. This dessert is often prepared weeks in advance, allowing the flavors to deepen and develop over time. In this air fryer recipe, we will be making a delicious Christmas pudding that is quick and easy to prepare, while still retaining all the classic flavors of this beloved dessert.

Prep time: 15 minutes | Cook time: about 4 hours| Serves 6

- 200g raisins
- 200g currants
- 100g chopped mixed peel
- 100g chopped dried apricots
- 100g plain flour
- 100g breadcrumbs
- 100g suet
- 100g light brown sugar
- 2 tsp mixed spice
- 1 tsp ground cinnamon
- 1 tsp ground ginger
- 1 apple, peeled and grated
- 2 large eggs
- 125ml stout or dark beer
- 2 tbsp brandy
- Zest and juice of 1 orange
- Zest and juice of 1 lemon
- For the topping:
- 50g plain flour
- 50g butter, softened
- 50g light brown sugar

1. In a large mixing bowl, combine the raisins, currants, mixed peel, apricots, flour, breadcrumbs, suet, sugar, mixed spice, cinnamon, ginger, and grated apple.
2. In another bowl, whisk together the eggs, stout or beer, brandy, orange zest and juice, and lemon zest and juice. Pour this mixture over the dry ingredients and mix well.
3. Grease a 1-liter pudding basin and spoon in the mixture. Cover the basin with a double layer of foil, pleating it in the center to allow room for expansion, and tie it tightly with string.
4. Place the pudding basin in the air fryer basket and cook at 150°C for 4 hours.
5. Meanwhile, make the topping by mixing the flour, butter, and sugar together in a bowl until crumbly.
6. After 4 hours, carefully remove the pudding basin from the air fryer and remove the foil. Sprinkle the topping over the pudding and return it to the air fryer for a further 20 minutes at 180°C, or until the topping is golden brown and the pudding is heated through.
7. Remove the pudding from the air fryer and let it cool for a few minutes before turning it out onto a plate. Serve with cream or brandy butter, if desired. Enjoy!

Turkey Recipe (Metric)

Here is an air fryer recipe for a delicious and juicy roasted turkey, perfect for any holiday or special occasion. Using the metric measurement, this recipe will guide you through the steps to cook a flavorful turkey in the air fryer, complete with crispy skin and tender, moist meat. Give this recipe a try and impress your family and friends with a perfectly cooked turkey!

Prep time: 15 minutes | Cook time: 1 hour 25 minutes| Serves 6

- 1 whole turkey (3-4 kg)
- 3 tbsp unsalted butter, softened
- 1 tbsp chopped fresh thyme
- 1 tbsp chopped fresh rosemary
- 1 tbsp chopped fresh sage
- 1 tsp garlic powder
- 1 tsp onion powder
- Salt and pepper to taste

1. Preheat your air fryer to 375°F (190°C).
2. Remove the turkey from its packaging and rinse it under cold water, then pat dry with paper towels.
3. In a small bowl, mix together the softened butter, thyme, rosemary, sage, garlic powder, onion powder, salt, and pepper.
4. Rub the herb butter all over the turkey, making sure to get it in between the skin and the meat as well.
5. Place the turkey in the air fryer basket breast side up.
6. Cook the turkey for 20 minutes per kg, so a 3 kg turkey will take around 60 minutes.
7. After 30 minutes, flip the turkey over and continue cooking.
8. Check the temperature of the turkey in the thickest part of the breast and thigh with a meat thermometer. The turkey should be cooked to an internal temperature of 165°F (75°C).
9. Once the turkey is fully cooked, let it rest for 10-15 minutes before carving.
10. Enjoy your delicious air-fried turkey!

Mince Pies Recipe (Metric)

Mince pies are a quintessential holiday dessert that are enjoyed by many during the festive season. This classic pastry is filled with a sweet and spiced mixture of dried fruits and suet, creating a warm and comforting flavor that's perfect for the colder months. With this air fryer recipe, you can make your own delicious and flaky mince pies at home with ease. The air fryer ensures that the pastry is crispy and golden while the filling is soft and gooey. Serve these warm mince pies with a dollop of whipped cream or a scoop of vanilla ice cream for the ultimate holiday treat.

Prep time: 15 minutes | Cook time: 20 minutes| Serves 4

- 300g plain flour
- 200g cold unsalted butter, cubed
- 50g caster sugar
- 1 egg yolk
- 1 tbsp cold water
- 400g mincemeat
- Icing sugar, for dusting

1. Preheat the air fryer to 180°C.
2. In a large bowl, mix the flour, butter and caster sugar together until it forms fine breadcrumbs. Add the egg yolk and cold water, and mix until a dough is formed.
3. Roll out the dough on a lightly floured surface to around 3mm thickness.
4. Using a round pastry cutter, cut out circles of dough to fit your muffin tin. Place each circle of dough in the muffin tin, pressing down lightly to make sure it fits snugly in the base.
5. Spoon 1-2 teaspoons of mincemeat into each pastry case.
6. Using the remaining dough, cut out smaller circles to form the pie lids. Place these on top of the mincemeat, pressing down lightly around the edges to seal.
7. Place the mince pies in the air fryer basket and cook for 10-12 minutes, until the pastry is golden brown.
8. Remove from the air fryer and allow to cool before dusting with icing sugar.
9. Enjoy your delicious and easy-to-make air fryer mince pies!

Brussels Sprouts (Metric)

Brussels sprouts are a classic vegetable that often makes an appearance on the holiday table. But with this air fryer recipe, you can enjoy them any time of the year! Roasting Brussels sprouts in an air fryer gives them a crispy texture on the outside while keeping them tender on the inside. Plus, this recipe is easy to customize with your favorite seasonings, making it a versatile side dish for any meal.

Prep time: 5 minutes | Cook time: 15 minutes| Serves 4

- 500g Brussels sprouts
- 3 tbsp olive oil
- 1 tsp garlic powder
- 1 tsp onion powder
- 1/2 tsp salt
- 1/4 tsp black pepper

1. Preheat your air fryer to 200°C.
2. Rinse the Brussels sprouts and cut off the stems. Cut them in half.
3. In a mixing bowl, combine olive oil, garlic powder, onion powder, salt, and black pepper. Mix well.
4. Add the Brussels sprouts to the bowl and mix until they are evenly coated with the seasoning.
5. Place the Brussels sprouts in the air fryer basket, making sure they are not overcrowded.
6. Cook the Brussels sprouts in the air fryer for 10-12 minutes, shaking the basket every 3-4 minutes to ensure even cooking.
7. Remove the Brussels sprouts from the air fryer and serve hot.
8. Enjoy your crispy and flavorful air fryer Brussels sprouts as a side dish with your roast dinner!

Appendix 3 Index

KATHRYNE R. BROOKS

Printed in Great Britain
by Amazon